# IDEAS

## NCTM Standards-Based Instruction

## Instruction

### Grades K–4

# IDEAS
## NCTM Standards-Based Instruction

Grades K–4

Compiled and edited

by

## Michael C. Hynes
University of Central Florida
Orlando, Florida

National Council of Teachers of Mathematics
Reston, Virginia

The special contents of this book are
Copyright © 1995 by
THE NATIONAL COUNCIL OF TEACHERS OF MATHEMATICS, INC.
1906 Association Drive, Reston, VA 20191-1593
All rights reserved

Second printing 1997

Library of Congress Cataloging-in-Publication Data:

Ideas : NCTM standards-based instruction : grades K–4 / compiled and
    edited by Michael C. Hynes.
        p.       cm.
    "These lessons have been selected from the 'Ideas' department in
    the Arithmetic teacher: mathematics education through the middle
    grades"—T.p. verso.
    Includes bibliographical references.
    ISBN 0-87353-422-0 (pbk.)
    1. Mathematics—Study and teaching (Elementary)    I. Hynes,
Michael C., 1941–   .    II. Arithmetic teacher.
QA135.5.I34  1995
372.7′044—dc20                                                    95-44215
                                                                         CIP

These lessons have been selected from the "Ideas" department in the
*Arithmetic Teacher: Mathematics Education through the Middle Grades.*

Printed in the United States of America

# Grade Levels and Publication Dates for "Ideas" Activities

| Activity | Date of Publication | K | 1 | 2 | 3 | 4 | Page Number |
|---|---|---|---|---|---|---|---|
| Stones for the Postman's Palace | April 94 | • | | | | | 4 |
| Love Stamps | April 94 | | • | • | • | | 6 |
| How Mail Moves | April 94 | | | | • | • | 8 |
| Beverage Sharing and Serving | February 94 | • | • | • | • | | 10 |
| Measurement Scavenger Hunt | January 94 | • | • | • | • | | 12 |
| What Can You Build with Two Triangles? | November 93 | • | • | | | | 14 |
| How Do You Build Triangles? | November 93 | | | • | • | | 16 |
| Graphing Trash Material | September 93 | • | • | | | | 18 |
| Classroom Paper | September 93 | | | • | • | • | 20 |
| Buttons! Buttons! | May 93 | • | • | | | | 22 |
| Shapes Art | May 93 | | | • | • | | 24 |
| Sorting SKITTLES/Graphing SKITTLES | April 93 | • | • | • | • | | 26 |
| Geometric Art | March 93 | • | • | • | | | 28 |
| Shapely Art | March 93 | | | • | • | • | 30 |
| Picturing Our Building | February 93 | • | • | • | | | 32 |
| Building with Newspaper Dowels | February 93 | | | | • | • | 34 |
| Figuring in Football | January 93 | • | • | | | | 36 |
| Get the Picture—Get the Story | January 93 | | | • | • | • | 38 |
| The Rhythm of Counting | December 92 | • | • | • | | | 40 |
| Measuring Music | December 92 | | | | • | • | 42 |
| Which Flavor Wins the Taste Test? | November 92 | • | • | • | | | 44 |
| You Are the Pollster | November 92 | | | | • | • | 46 |
| Exploring a Community | October 92 | • | • | • | | | 48 |
| Getting to Know You | September 92 | • | • | • | | | 50 |
| Have a Seat | September 92 | | | | • | • | 52 |
| Computation Court: You Be the Judge | May 92 | • | • | • | • | | 54 |
| Hop to It! | April 92 | • | • | • | | | 56 |
| Long Leaps for Olympic Gold | April 92 | | | • | • | • | 58 |
| Numbers on a Kite Tail | March 92 | • | • | • | | | 60 |
| Pin the Tail on the Kite | March 92 | | | | • | • | 62 |
| How Big Is Your Heart? | February 92 | • | • | • | | | 64 |
| Every Beat of Your Heart | February 92 | | | | • | • | 66 |
| Discovering Figures | January 92 | • | • | • | | | 68 |
| Geometric Figures | January 92 | | | | • | • | 70 |
| Toy-Shop Numbers | December 91 | • | • | • | | | 72 |
| Post-Office Numbers | December 91 | | | | • | • | 74 |
| Cut to Create | November 91 | • | • | • | | | 76 |
| Create a New Figure | November 91 | | | | • | • | 78 |
| What's the Weather? | October 91 | • | • | • | | | 80 |
| Numbers and Me | September 91 | • | • | • | • | | 82 |
| Survey of Hair and Eye Colors | September 91 | | | • | • | • | 84 |
| Favorite Television Programs | May 91 | | • | • | • | • | 86 |
| Pizza-Topping Combinations | April 91 | • | • | • | • | • | 88 |
| Favorite Pizza Toppings | April 91 | | • | • | • | • | 90 |
| Thumbprint Graph | March 91 | | • | • | • | | 92 |

# Acknowledgments

The lessons selected for this publication are taken from original "Ideas" activities prepared and edited by the following:

Dianne Bankard

Anne F. Brahier

Daniel J. Brahier

Emalou Brumfield

Marea W. Channel

Rebecca B. Corwin

Yvonne M. Coston

Francis (Skip) Fennell

John Firkins

Diane M. Gard

Shirley Hodapp

Martha H. (Marty) Hopkins

Calvin Irons

Rosemary Irons

J. David Keller

Beth Kobett

Rebecca Martin

L. J. Meconi

Phyllis Knerl Miller

Barbara E. Moses

Mary Lou Nevin

Karen S. Norwood

Lisa M. Passarello

Linda Proudfit

Sherry Renga

Kay B. Sammons

Jean M. Shaw

Robert Sovchik

William R. Speer

Danna Stonecipher

Virginia Usnick

Sharon L. Young

The preparation of this manuscript was made possible through the cooperation of the Department of Instructional Programs at the University of Central Florida. Kathleen Frey provided editorial assistance and graphics preparation for drafts of the publication. Lucy Roberts was an editorial assistant throughout the project. Their efforts contributed to the quality and timely completion of this publication.

# Introduction

Consistently since its inception in 1971, the "Ideas" department has been ranked as one of the most popular features of the *Arithmetic Teacher*. When the journal became known as *Arithmetic Teacher: Mathematics Education through the Middle Grades*, the popularity of "Ideas" continued. Readers of the journal find the format of activity sheets and teacher directions to be very helpful in preparing lessons. Many readers report that they often copy the activity sheets for direct use in the classroom.

Early in the development of "Ideas," the lessons focused on creative paper-and-pencil activities. These lessons were intended to be used to augment the textbook and make lessons more exciting. As the reform movement in mathematics education began, the feature evolved to new levels. The use of manipulatives became an important part of the lessons, and children were encouraged to use higher-order-thinking skills.

The publication of NCTM's *Curriculum and Evaluation Standards for School Mathematics* in 1989 added new aspects to the department. Without losing the friendly format, "Ideas" lessons incorporated communication, connections, reasoning, and problem solving. Teachers saw examples of how to teach statistics and probability in the primary grades through "Ideas" lessons that use data sheets. In the later volumes of *Arithmetic Teacher: Mathematics Education through the Middle Grades*, teachers were given assistance in communicating with parents when Family Activities were included.

This collection of "Ideas" lessons has been compiled from the 1991–94 journals. The lessons selected were indicated by authors to be appropriate for grades K–4. The activity sheets have been edited for clarity, and because of space limitations the teacher directions may have been edited for brevity. For the reader's immediate reference, the issue of the journal in which the original lesson appeared is noted at the bottom of the activity sheet. Family Activities and Data Sheets have been placed in separate sections. The teacher directions indicate if there is a corresponding page in these special sections.

For the reader's convenience, two reference pages are included in this publication. The first reference page is a matrix of the titles of the activities, the date of publication, and the intended grade levels for each of the activities. This page will be helpful to the teacher looking for activities for a particular grade level. Also, many teachers are seeking examples of how to incorporate ideas from the *Standards* into their lessons. The second reference page correlates the titles of the activities with the NCTM Standards. Since many of the "Ideas" lessons involve multiple standards, teachers should review the lessons carefully to be certain that the desired emphasis on a particular standard is present.

| Activity | Problem Solving | Communication | Reasoning | Connections | Estimation | Number Sense and Numeration | Concepts of Whole-Number Operations | Whole-Number Operations | Geometry and Spatial Sense | Measurement | Statistics and Probability | Fractions and Decimals | Patterns and Relationships | Page Number |
|---|---|---|---|---|---|---|---|---|---|---|---|---|---|---|
| Stones for the Postman's Palace | | | | • | | | | | • | | | | | 4 |
| Love Stamps | | | • | • | | • | | • | | | | | | 6 |
| How Mail Moves | | | • | • | | | | | | | | | | 8 |
| Beverage Sharing and Serving | | | | • | | • | • | | | • | | | | 10 |
| Measurement Scavenger Hunt | | | | • | • | | | | | • | | | | 12 |
| What Can You Build with Two Triangles? | • | | • | | | | | | • | | | | | 14 |
| How Do You Build Triangles? | • | | • | | | | | | • | | | | | 16 |
| Graphing Trash Material | | • | | • | • | | | | | | • | | | 18 |
| Classroom Paper | | • | | • | • | | | | | | • | | | 20 |
| Buttons! Buttons! | | • | • | | | • | | | | | | | | 22 |
| Shapes Art | | • | | • | | | | | • | | | | | 24 |
| Sorting SKITTLES/Graphing SKITTLES | | • | | • | • | • | | | | | • | | | 26 |
| Geometric Art | | • | • | | | | | | • | | | | | 28 |
| Shapely Art | | | • | | | | | | • | | | | | 30 |
| Picturing Our Building | | • | | | | • | | | • | | | | | 32 |
| Building with Newspaper Dowels | | • | | | | • | | | • | | | | | 34 |
| Figuring in Football | • | | | | | | | | • | | | | | 36 |
| Get the Picture—Get the Story | • | • | | • | | • | • | | | • | | | | 38 |
| The Rhythm of Counting | | | | • | | • | | | | | | | • | 40 |
| Measuring Music | • | | | • | | | | | | • | | • | | 42 |
| Which Flavor Wins the Taste Test? | | | | • | | | | • | | | • | | | 44 |
| You Are the Pollster | • | • | | • | | | | | | | • | | | 46 |
| Exploring a Community | • | | | • | | | | | • | | | | | 48 |
| Getting to Know You | | | | | | • | | | | | • | | • | 50 |
| Have a Seat | • | • | | • | | • | | | • | | | | • | 52 |
| Computation Court: You Be the Judge | • | • | • | | | | • | • | | | | | | 54 |
| Hop to It! | | • | | | • | | | | | • | | | | 56 |
| Long Leaps for Olympic Gold | | | | • | • | • | | | | • | • | • | | 58 |
| Numbers on a Kite Tail | | | | | | • | | | | | | | | 60 |
| Pin the Tail on the Kite | | | | | | • | • | • | | | | | | 62 |
| How Big Is Your Heart? | | | | • | | | | | | • | | | | 64 |
| Every Beat of Your Heart | • | | | • | | • | | | | | • | | | 66 |
| Discovering Figures | | | • | • | | | | | • | | | | | 68 |
| Geometric Figures | • | | | | | | | | • | | | | • | 70 |
| Toy-Shop Numbers | | • | | | | • | • | | | | | | | 72 |
| Post-Office Numbers | | • | | • | | • | | | | | | • | | 74 |
| Cut to Create | • | | | | | | | | • | | | | | 76 |
| Create a New Figure | • | • | | | | | | | • | | | | | 78 |
| What's the Weather? | | | | • | | • | • | | | | • | | | 80 |
| Numbers and Me | | | | • | | • | | | | | | | | 82 |
| Survey of Hair and Eye Colors | | | | • | | | | | | | • | • | | 84 |
| Favorite Television Programs | | • | | | | • | | | | | • | | | 86 |
| Pizza-Topping Combinations | • | | | | | • | • | | | | | | | 88 |
| Favorite Pizza Toppings | | • | | | | | | | | | • | | | 90 |
| Thumbprint Graph | • | • | | | | | | | | | | | • | 92 |

IDEAS

Activity Sheets

# Stones for the Postman's Palace

## LEVELS PRE-K–K

### Literature

Henri, Adrian. *The Postman's Palace.* New York: Atheneum Publishers, 1990.

### Background

In the book *The Postman's Palace* a mail carrier observed many interesting stones of various shapes and sizes as he carried mail on his route. Over a period of years, he collected stones that intrigued him. When he had a sufficient number of stones, he used them to build a palace.

### Objectives

The pupils design figures on paper to represent stones, then model their figures in three dimensions using play dough. They cooperatively build a palace using their creations.

### Directions

1. Read aloud *The Postman's Palace* and discuss the various shapes portrayed in the book. Ask students if they would like to make their own palace like the postman's palace.

2. Distribute a copy of the activity sheet "Stones for the Postman's Palace" to each student. Read the instructions to the class. Ask each student to design one stone on the activity sheet. Then hand out play dough and have the students use play dough to make the stones they designed.

3. Guide the students in cooperatively building a palace using a large set of blocks and their play-dough stones.

### Applicable Standards

- **Connections**
- **Geometry and Spatial Sense**

*Prepared by* Sherry Renga
*Edited by* John Firkins

IDEAS

Name _____

# Stones for the Postman's Palace

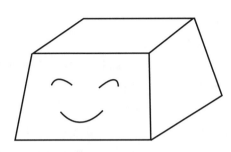

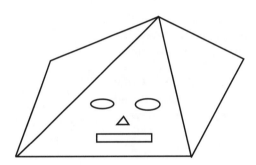

Here are some stones for the postman's palace. Design your own stone below, then make a play-dough model of your stone.

From the *Arithmetic Teacher*, April 1994

# IDEAS

# Love Stamps

## LEVELS 1–3

### Literature

Jacobsen, Karen. *Stamps*. Chicago: Childrens Press, 1983.

United States Postal Service. *The Postal Service Guide to U.S. Stamps*. Washington, D.C.: The Service, 1992.

Zeigler, Sandra. *A Visit to the Post Office*. Chicago: Childrens Press, 1989.

### Background

February is a good time to use this activity. The love stamps shown on the activity sheet are first-class stamps issued in the years indicated. The 1992 stamp is reproduced from an actual stamp. The other stamps, reproduced on the activity sheet in order by year, are from *The Postal Service Guide to U.S. Stamps* (pp. 159, 227, 235, 240, 247, 260, 271, and 279) .

### Objectives

Pupils become familiar with stamps, their purpose, and their cost, with an emphasis on one type of stamp. Pupils compare the differences in prices over twenty years and investigate why the prices of stamps have increased during this time.

### Directions

1. Distribute a copy of the activity sheet "Love Stamps" to each pupil. Divide the class into groups of four.

2. Have each group describe the stamps on the activity sheet then share their descriptions with the entire class. Discuss why the illustrations on the stamps are considered appropriate for "love" stamps; how does each stamp relate to the term *love?* Responses might include the following: "We give roses to those we love." "The love doves are a symbol for love." (Why?) "Love makes the world go 'round."

3. Work together as a whole class to complete the activity sheet. For younger children, you may wish to use play money on a flannel board to demonstrate the cost of the stamps and the differences in prices among the years given. With older children, you may wish to compare the changes in the prices of stamps with the rate of inflation over the given period.

### Extensions

1. Decorate a February bulletin board using the love stamps designed by the children.

2. Read aloud *A Visit to the Post Office*. Schedule a field trip to your local post office, following the same format as that used in the book.

3. Read aloud *Stamps*. If any of the children have an interest in stamp collecting, this book can help get them started.

### Applicable Standards

- **Reasoning**
- **Connections**
- **Number Sense and Numeration**
- **Whole-Number Operations**

### Answers

1. 20 cents
2. 2 cents, 3 cents, 0 cents, 4 cents
3. 1990 to 1992; 1988 to 1990; answers will vary.
4. 21 cents
5. Answers will vary.

*Prepared by* Sherry Renga
*Edited by* John Firkins

Name _____

# Love Stamps

1973

1984

1985

1986

1987

1988

1990

1991

1992

1. How much did the 1984 stamp cost? _____

2. How much did the price increase from 1984 to 1986? _____
   From 1986 to 1988? _____
   From 1988 to 1990? _____
   From 1990 to 1992? _____

3. In question 2, during what two-year time span did the price increase the most? _____
   The least? _____
   Why do you think the prices increased when and as much as they did? _____

4. What is the overall increase in the price of the love stamp from 1973 to 1992? _____

5. Why do you think the prices of stamps keep increasing rather than decreasing? _____

6. Design your own love stamp in the space below.

From the *Arithmetic Teacher*, April 1994

# How Mail Moves

## LEVELS 3–4

### Literature

Gibbons, Gail. *The Post Office Book: Mail and How It Moves.* New York: Thomas Y. Crowell, 1982.

United States Postal Service. *National Five-Digit ZIP Code and Post Office Directory.* 2 vols. Washington, D.C.: The Service, 1992.

### Background

*The Post Office Book: Mail and How It Moves* is written at an appropriate level for grades K–4. The book describes how mail moves within a post office and among various post offices.

A United States ZIP code is a numerical code that identifies specific areas within the United States and its territories to assist in the distribution of mail by the United States Postal Service. The leftmost digit of a United States ZIP code divides the country into ten large groups of states numbered from 0 in the northeast to 9 in the west. Within the large groups of states, each state is parceled into smaller geographical areas; these are identified by the second and third digits of the ZIP code. The two rightmost digits of the ZIP code identify a local delivery area (United States Postal Service 1992, 1-1). The United States Postal Service has created and implemented ZIP + 4 codes. The first two digits of the four-digit add-on code identify a delivery sector, and the last two digits identify a delivery segment. The purpose of the additional four digits is to allow computerized machinery to sort mail to a finer degree (United States Postal Service 1992, 10-1).

A Canadian postal code is composed of both letters and numerals. The leftmost character is a letter that denotes the province. The second character is a numeral that identifies the area by size from rural to urban; 0 indicates a rural area. The third character indicates a small unit within the area. The fourth character shows the point of delivery; the letter carrier sorts the mail delivery at this location. The street name is indicated by the fifth character, and the street number is shown by the sixth character.

### Objectives

The students use information from literature and a map to conjecture about how mail travels from one place to another. They use reasoning skills to arrange the events of travel in a logical sequence.

### Directions

1. Read aloud and discuss *The Post Office Book: Mail and How It Moves.*

2. Place students in groups of four. Distribute a copy of the worksheet "How Mail Moves" to each student and discuss the activity with the class. Include a discussion of ZIP codes. Ask the students what their ZIP codes are; are they the same for all class members? What is the significance of the first two digits of a United States ZIP code? Some ZIP codes now have an additional four digits added; for what are these numerals used?

3. Guide the students in locating the cities and towns named on the activity sheet on a map of the United States and Canada. Discuss their ideas about how the letter shown might reach its destination.

(Mail from Friday Harbor, Washington, is sent either by airplane or by ferry to Everett, Washington. If the weather is clear, the mail goes by airplane; if the sky is overcast, it goes by ferry. The mail is taken by truck from Everett to an airplane at the Seattle airport and sent to Calgary. From Calgary, it is trucked to Banff. No street delivery is available in Banff, so mail is distributed through general delivery or in a box at the post office.) *Note:* Some students may not be aware that a letter can be mailed from their own mailbox. You may want to add this information to the discussion.

4. After discussing the activity sheet, have the groups complete the activity. Additional cut-out squares from a second activity sheet may be needed. Discuss the results.

### Answer

Answers may vary. One possibility is the following: The use of small trucks, large trucks, and airplanes will vary depending on the location. One possible answer is H-J-C-I-D-E-K-G-F-A. The sequence could begin with B or H.

*Prepared by* Sherry Renga
*Edited by* John Firkins

---

### Applicable Standards

- **Reasoning**
- **Connections**

# How Mail Moves

Cut out the squares lettered A through K. Arrange them to show how the letter shown at the left below will travel to its destination.

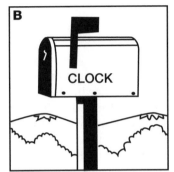

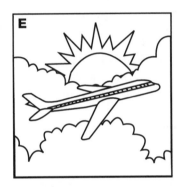

From the *Arithmetic Teacher*, April 1994

# Beverage Sharing and Serving

## LEVELS K–3

### Background

Students need to understand that serving crackers or a similar item to classmates at snack time involves a one-to-one correspondence between crackers served and students present. Students must be able to determine, by counting the students and the available crackers, whether the number of crackers available is greater than, less than, or equal to, the number of students present.

Students should have had some experience in pouring liquids from one container into another. They should also have developed some understanding of measurement using nonstandard units.

### Objectives

To determine, using a nonstandard cup or plastic drinking container, the minimum amount of a beverage needed to serve class members; to prepare and properly serve the beverage to each student

### Materials

- A ready-to-serve beverage in a sufficient quantity for approximately six ounces to be served to each student
- A chart for each group to record estimates
- An empty beverage container
- Several cups or plastic drinking containers of different capacities
- Water
- A bowl for dumping the water
- Paper or cloth towels

### Discussion

1. What should be the amount of ready-to-serve beverage that makes up one serving?

2. How can the beverage be shared so that each student receives the same amount?

3. Estimate and record the following information under Estimation in the table on the activity sheet "Beverage Sharing and Serving":

   *a)* How many servings can be poured from one container of the beverage?

   *b)* How many servings (one for each student) are required?

   *c)* How many containers of the beverage will be needed to serve all the students?

### Activities

1. Divide the students conveniently into small groups.

2. Using water to represent the beverage, have the students pour from the container and record the answers for the practice session under the column Water Practice in the table.

3. Will all the beverage from all opened containers be needed to serve the class? If not, how many servings will remain in the container? Estimate answers. What should be done with the leftover amount? Record your answers and give them to your teacher.

### Discussion

Ask the class to discuss and decide—

1. the day and time this beverage break will occur;

2. from where in the room the beverage will be served;

3. who will be responsible for opening the beverage containers, pouring the beverage from the original containers into pitchers or a punch bowl, arranging the proper number of drinking cups, ladling or pouring the beverage into cups, cleaning up after the activity, disposing of any leftover beverage, and other related duties.

Using water, practice pouring or ladling into a drinking cup the amount of beverage required for a serving.

With the knowledge and experience acquired by pouring and ladling, students should prepare and present their snack-time beverage to classmates in an enjoyable, equitable, and proper manner and complete the cleanup quietly and efficiently.

### Follow-up activities

1. Complete the right-hand column of the table on the activity sheet "Beverage Sharing and Serving," using the information gathered from snack time.

2. Discuss and compare the differences between and among the numbers in the three columns of your chart.

3. In what other situations might some or all of this activity help us plan and organize our work?

### Applicable Standards

- **Connections**
- **Number Sense and Numeration**
- **Concepts of Whole-Number Operations**
- **Measurement**

*Prepared by* Emalou Brumfield
*Edited by* John Firkins

# Beverage Sharing and Serving

| | Report of Group #_____ | | |
|---|---|---|---|
| | Estimation | Water practice | Actual servings |
| 1. Number of servings in one container | | | |
| 2. Number of servings required | | | |
| 3. Number of containers needed for class | | | |
| 4. Number of leftover servings | ✕ | | |

*From the Arithmetic Teacher, February 1994*

IDEAS

# Measurement Scavenger Hunt

## LEVELS K–3

### Background

Young students can gain valuable experience in using such fundamental units of measure as centimeters, meters, and grams, as well as nonstandard units, during a short walk near their school. A measurement scavenger hunt can help reinforce the learning of fundamental units of measure. Students can find items on a short list that meet specified measures. Later, they can discuss their findings in class and develop valuable communication skills as they share results.

### Objectives

To identify examples of items with predetermined measures; to communicate findings by justifying to class members the reasons for selection

### Directions

1. Duplicate the activity sheet "Measurement Scavenger Hunt" for each student.

2. Form groups of three to five students and give each group a list of items to find, such as those discussed on the "Measurement Scavenger Hunt" activity sheet. Have each team member measure the length of his or her thumbs, forefingers, and hands to provide an easy referent for the measurement tasks.

3. Lead the students on a short walk. Be sure the route takes them past trees, rocks, and twigs.

4. For younger students, discuss any items you find along the route that are suitable for the measurement activity. Older students can record the findings on the activity sheet.

5. Have a follow-up discussion so that students can explain their results. Ask students to justify and explain their findings.

---

### Applicable Standards

- **Connections**
- **Estimation**
- **Measurement**

---

### Extension

Repeat this activity using such customary units as inches, feet, and pounds. Use familiar items in the classroom as referents. Also, consider scheduling this activity during another season, perhaps in the autumn when leaves have fallen. Leaf patterns could serve as source material for your list of scavenger items. For example, direct the students to find a leaf with more than three points or one that has a rounded design. Have students estimate the weight of a bag of leaves, using a seesaw and a student whose weight is known.

---

*Prepared by* Robert Sovchik *and* L. J. Meconi
*Edited by* John Firkins

Name _____

# Measurement Scavenger Hunt

My thumb is _____ centimeters long. My hand is _____ centimeters long. My forefinger is _____ centimeters long.

Find a twig, a leaf, a rock, and a blade of grass to match each of the following measurements. Indicate approximately how many centimeters long each item is.

| Item | Longer than your hand (It is about this many centimeters long.) | Shorter than your thumb (It is about this many centimeters long.) | Longer than your forefinger but shorter than your hand (It is about this many centimeters long.) |
|---|---|---|---|
| Twig | _____ cm | _____ cm | _____ cm |
| Leaf | _____ cm | _____ cm | _____ cm |
| Rock | _____ cm | _____ cm | _____ cm |
| Blade of grass | _____ cm | _____ cm | _____ cm |
| A special item you found on your walk | _____ cm | _____ cm | _____ cm |

How many hands long is the longest twig you found? _____ How many cm long is it? _____

How many hands long is the longest blade of grass? _____ How many cm long is it? _____

Which tree on your walk is the oldest? Why do you think so? _____

_____

Find two leaves, one twice as big as the other. Why do you think it is twice as big? _____

_____

From the *Arithmetic Teacher*, January 1994

# What Can You Build with Two Triangles?

## LEVELS K–1

### Objective

Students explore ways to build different basic shapes from two triangles, then three or more triangles.

### Materials

- A copy of the activity sheet "What Can You Build with Two Triangles?" for each student
- Scissors, glue
- Duplicated models of a square, a triangle, and a parallelogram
- Masking tape for the extension activity 2

### Directions

1. Distribute the activity sheets.

2. Have students cut out two triangles from the activity sheet.

3. Use the models of the square, triangle, and parallelogram to encourage the students to make these shapes. Ask them to try to make these and other shapes with two triangles.

4. Ask the students to glue the "new" shapes onto the activity sheet.

5. Dictate or write a group letter to another class to let the students know that it is possible to make many shapes from triangles.

6. Encourage the students to share at least one important thing that they noticed about one of the new shapes: likenesses and differences; where it could be seen in the classroom, playground, school, or at home; and so on.

7. Enclose a copy of the activity sheet with the letter so that the receiving class can make its own investigations.

8. First graders might enjoy ending the letter with a question.

### Answers

The following are some possible answers:

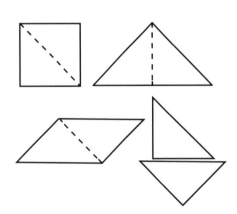

### Applicable Standards

- **Problem Solving**
- **Reasoning**
- **Geometry and Spatial Sense**

### Extensions

1. Ask students to build "new" shapes with three or more triangles.

2. Investigate building three-dimensional shapes with triangles. You will need to duplicate the triangles on heavy paper.

*Prepared by* Marea W. Channel
*Edited by* John Firkins

# What Can You Build with Two Triangles?

Can you build a ☐ ? A bigger △ ? What else can you build?

Cut out the triangles below. Build different shapes with two triangles. Glue your shapes in the frame above. Tell someone about your ideas.

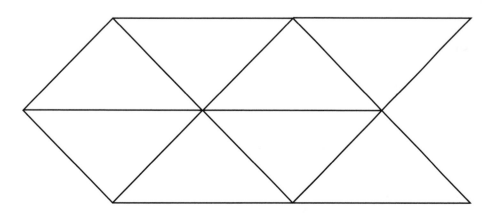

From the *Arithmetic Teacher*, November 1993

# How Do You Build Triangles?

## LEVELS 2–3

### Objectives

Students investigate properties of triangles and relationships among other geometric figures by putting pattern-block shapes together to make triangles. They develop mathematical language as they describe solutions.

### Materials

- A copy of the activity sheet "How Do You Build Triangles?" for each student. For best results, duplicate the sheet on construction paper.
- Triangular shapes of various sizes
- Pattern blocks. Omit the square and the white parallelogram.
- Scissors, glue
- Extra paper and activity sheets for the extension activity

### Directions

1. Display various triangular figures and ask, "How do you know that these figures are triangular?" The following properties of triangles should emerge from this discussion: three sides, three corners and angles, straight rather than curved sides.

2. Distribute pattern blocks to each group of two to four students.

3. Have students explore ways to make triangles with the pattern blocks.

4. Have students share solutions with one another.

5. Distribute and follow directions in the activity sheet "How Do You Build Triangles?"

6. Have the students work in pairs to give or write directions for building one of the triangles, then see if another pair of students can build it by following the directions.

### Answers

### Applicable Standards

- **Problem Solving**
- **Reasoning**
- **Geometry and Spatial Sense**

### Extension

Ask the students to use only the twelve shapes on the activity sheet to answer the following:

- How many different triangles can be built with two, three, and then four shapes?
- What happens if all twelve shapes are used to build one "huge" triangle? (One more small triangle is needed because the pattern for the triangular area is one, four, nine, sixteen, and twenty-five small triangles.)
- What is the largest triangle that can be built with twelve shapes?
- How many different symmetrical designs can be created for the largest triangle?

*Prepared by* Marea W. Channel
*Edited by* John Firkins

Name _____

# How Do You Build Triangles?

How many different triangles can you build with pattern-block shapes? To find out, cut out the pattern-block shapes below. Give your solutions in the frame.

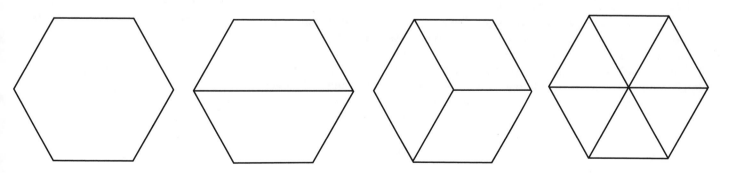

From the *Arithmetic Teacher*, November 1993

IDEAS

# Graphing Trash Material

## LEVELS K–1

### Background

Most students discard items in the classroom without thinking about what kinds of materials they are throwing away. This activity increases students' awareness of the number and kinds of materials they discard. It also encourages them to think about taking action by reusing and recycling some of these items.

### Objective

To gain experience in gathering and categorizing data and making and interpreting graphs to develop an action plan

### Directions

1. Let students work in groups of twos or threes. Have each group save materials they would ordinarily throw away. They can also pick through the classroom trash and select clean, safe items.

2. Have each group pick ten trash items at random. Lead a discussion on the kinds of materials the students have selected. Paper and plastic items will be common, but plastic foam, wood, cloth, metal, and items made of two or more materials—paper and plastic packaging for pencils, for example—may also be found.

3. Distribute a copy of the "Graphing Trash Material" activity sheet to each group. Read the title and captions. Help students decide on, and write names for, the remaining categories on the graph. You might want to title one of these categories "Other."

4. Have the students predict how many items will be in each category. Students can record their predictions on the sheet.

5. Help students count their trash materials and fill in the appropriate number of spaces for each category. Have each group report its results to another group and compare their findings. As they work, circulate and see what kinds of things they are discussing. Prompt them as necessary to notice categories with no items, categories with equal numbers of items, and so on.

6. Lay the graphs on the floor or on a table. Have students gather around them as you or a group member finish counting the number of items in each category. Compare the totals with the predictions.

7. Discuss some of the trash items that could be reused or recycled. Let each group draw pictures on the activity sheet of ways to reuse or recycle some of the items. Have a representative of each group show and tell what the group has decided.

8. Use some of the students' ideas for reusing and recycling materials if possible.

### Answers

Answers will vary according to the materials the students find. Spot check their counting and abilities to discuss their findings. Recognize practical and creative ideas for reusing and recycling materials.

### Applicable Standards

- **Communication**
- **Connections**
- **Estimation**
- **Statistics and Probability**

### Extensions

1. Have students choose ten trash items on another day, graph them according to category of material, and compare the two graphs.

2. Have students implement some of their ideas for reusing materials. Display the results and pictures in a place where others can see them.

3. Have each student bring ten clean, safe trash items from home. Discuss possible differences between trash items from home and school. Have students graph their home trash and compare their results with their previously made graphs of classroom trash.

4. Discuss other ways to categorize and graph trash materials. Students can use some of these ways to arrange trash items on a bulletin-board graph or floor graph.

### Family activity

See "Plastic Packaging" on page 104.

*Prepared by* Jean M. Shaw
*Edited by* John Firkins

# Graphing Trash Material

Name ____________________

What Is in Our Trash?

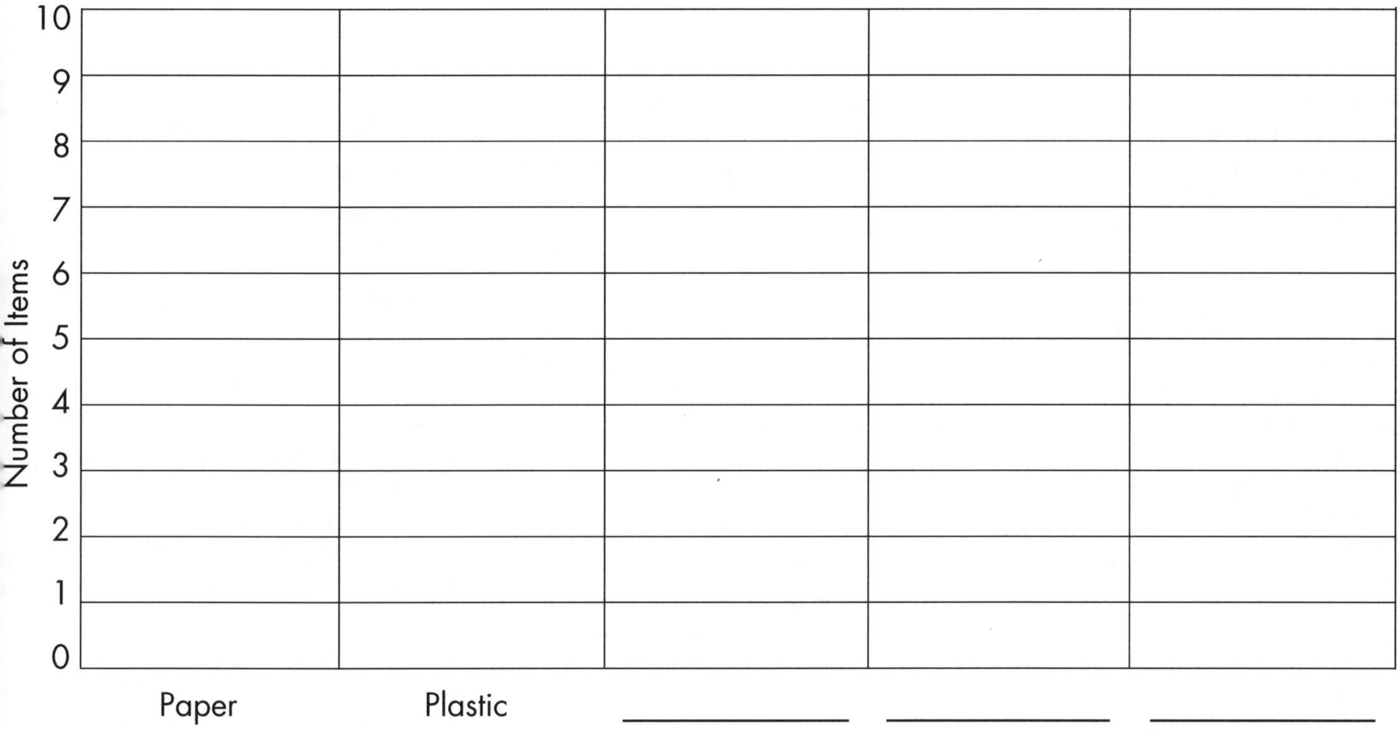


Write your prediction of how many items will be found.

__________ __________ __________ __________ __________

Write the actual number of each item that was found.

__________ __________ __________ __________ __________

Draw ways to recycle or reuse some of our trash.

From the *Arithmetic Teacher*, September 1993

# IDEAS

# Classroom Paper

## LEVELS 2–4

### Background

Using paper is a traditional part of classroom life. Efforts to conserve may start with a careful look at paper use. This activity requires students to keep track of their own paper use for a week then interpret their results with partners. After studying information on paper use, students will be ready to discuss ideas and implement plans for saving paper in the classroom.

### Objectives

To gather and graph information over a period of several days; to interpret information found in a graph and use the data as a basis for future planning

### Directions

1. Introduce the "Classroom Paper" activity sheet early in the day, perhaps on a Monday. Ask students about the many ways they use paper in the classroom.

2. Have them record on the activity sheet their predictions for the number of pieces of paper each will use during the day. Help students date each entry.

3. Students should keep the activity sheet available during the day and record a tally mark each time they use a sheet of paper.

4. At the end of the day, have students count their tally marks and fill in the graph to indicate the number of pieces of paper used.

5. Each day for the next four days, have students repeat steps 2–4. They may want to consider their estimates on the basis of the results of the previous days.

6. When the data collection and graphs are completed, have each student work with a partner. They should exchange graphs and answer question 1. Next, each partner should write questions in space 2 for the other to answer in space 3.

7. Discuss some of the observations, questions, and answers. Have each student answer question 4 and share the answer with a small group.

8. Discuss the findings in general. Were the results surprising? Do students think they are using too much paper? What are some ideas for saving paper?

9. Have each student write a plan for saving paper in the classroom in the space provided. Encourage implementation.

### Answers

Answers will vary. Spot-check the students' work to see that the numbers shown on the graph and recorded as actual numbers match their tallies. As they work on items 2–4, circulate and listen. Encourage them to check the reasonableness and accuracy of each other's questions and answers. Check to see that each student has made some sort of plan for saving paper.

### Extensions

1. Appoint a committee of students to make a poster based on some of the suggestions for saving paper. Display the poster in the classroom or present it to another class.

2. After a week or two, have students complete another graph on paper use to compare those graph results with the previous ones. Answer such questions as these: Is the number of pieces of paper you used before and after you implemented your plan different? How do you know? On the basis of what you found, would you say your plan for saving paper in the classroom is working? Why or why not?

3. Have groups examine and compare their graphs and discuss things they notice. For example, why might numbers vary from student to student? Why might some days' graphs show everyone using more pieces or fewer pieces of paper than on other days? Have group members share an interesting idea with the class.

### Family activity

See "Plastic Packaging" on page 104.

**Applicable Standards**

- **Communication**
- **Connections**
- **Estimation**
- **Statistics and Probability**

*Prepared by* Jean M. Shaw
*Edited by* John Firkins

# Classroom Paper

Name _____

### Pieces of Paper Used Each Day

| Prediction | Tally | Date | | Actual Number |
|---|---|---|---|---|
| _____ | _____ | _____ | | _____ |
| _____ | _____ | _____ | | _____ |
| _____ | _____ | _____ | | _____ |
| _____ | _____ | _____ | | _____ |
| _____ | _____ | _____ | | _____ |

0    2    4    6    8    10    12
                                    or more

Number of pieces of paper

1. What does the graph tell you? _____

_____

_____

2. Write some questions about the graph. _____

_____

_____

3. Let your partner answer your questions. _____

_____

_____

4. What did you learn from this project? _____

_____

_____

5. This is my plan for saving paper at school: _____

_____

_____

From the *Arithmetic Teacher*, September 1993

# IDEAS

# Buttons! Buttons!

## LEVELS K–1

### Literature

Lobel, Arnold. "A Lost Button." In *Frog and Toad Are Friends*. New York: HarperCollins Publishers, 1970. ISBN 0-06-444020-6.

### Story summary

Toad has lost a button and Frog helps him look for it. During the search, several buttons are found, but each time, Toad tells Frog why that button is *not* his button. After a frustrated Toad goes home empty handed, he finds his button lying on the floor of his own home! He makes a special gift for his friend Frog.

### Objective

Students use clues when sorting and classifying.

### Materials

- *Frog and Toad Are Friends* by Arnold Lobel
- A copy of the "Buttons! Buttons!" activity sheet for each student
- Sets of black, white, large, small, thick, thin, square, round, two-hole, and four-hole buttons (optional)
- Crayons

### Directions

1. Read the entire story aloud.

2. To small groups of students, distribute bags of buttons, one of which fits the description of Toad's button.

3. Direct the students to empty the bags onto their tables. Reread the story, stopping after each description Toad provides to allow students to eliminate buttons that couldn't possibly be Toad's.

4. At the conclusion of the reading, one button should remain. Ask students to describe the remaining button. (Steps 2–4 are optional.)

5. Distribute a copy of the "Buttons! Buttons!" activity sheet to each student.

6. Direct the students to cross off buttons that Toad says are *not* his after carefully reading each of the clues at the top of the page. After the final clue is read, one button that is not crossed off should remain on the activity sheet.

7. Ask the students to describe the remaining button in the space provided.

### Applicable Standards

- **Communication**
- **Reasoning**
- **Number Sense and Numeration**

8. Encourage the students to discuss how they eliminated groups of buttons; for example, if the button is not black, it must be white.

9. Check the activity sheet by rereading the story.

### Extension

Give the students a collection of buttons. Ask them to choose one of the buttons secretly and to hold a class discussion to help others guess which button they have selected.

### Family activity

See "Making Beds" on page 106.

*Prepared by* Martha H. (Marty) Hopkins
*Edited by* William R. Speer *and* Daniel J. Brahier

# Buttons! Buttons!

Toad has lost his button, and Frog is trying to help him find it. Can you help Frog find Toad's button? Here are some clues:

> The button is *not* black.          The button does *not* have two holes.
> The button is *not* small.          The button is *not* thin.
> The button is *not* square.

Which button is Toad's?

Describe Toad's button. _____

_____

_____

From the *Arithmetic Teacher*, May 1993

# Shapes Art

## Literature

Silverstein, Shel. "Shapes." In *A Light in the Attic*. New York: Harper & Row, Publishers, 1981. ISBN 0-06-025673-7.

## Poem summary

A square is minding its own business when a triangle comes down and strikes the square in the back. A circle comes to the square's rescue.

## Objectives

Students recognize, draw, and describe geometric figures. Students interpret positional words.

## Materials

- *A Light in the Attic* by Shel Silverstein
- A copy of the "Shapes Art" activity sheet for each student
- One each of a square, rectangle, triangle, and circle from attribute materials for each student (optional)

## Directions

1. Read the entire poem aloud.

2. Distribute attribute shapes to each student. Direct them to arrange their shapes according to what they hear in the poem. Reread the poem several times, giving students the opportunity to check their placements (optional).

3. Distribute copies of the "Shapes Art" activity sheet

4. If the students have already arranged the attribute materials, direct them to copy their arrangement under the heading "My Illustration." If attribute materials are not used, direct students to read the poem carefully and then illustrate it under "My Illustration" on the sheet.

5. After the students complete the drawing, direct them to justify their illustrations and then to share them with each other. Encourage them to "argue" their case. (Remind the students that it is possible that a wide variety of illustrations will be drawn that are all entirely justifiable.)

6. Complete the remainder of the activity sheet.

## Applicable Standards

- **Communication**
- **Connections**
- **Geometry and Spatial Sense**

## Extension

Supply students with several other shapes. Encourage them to write a poem or story using the shapes. As the stories are shared, ask other class members to illustrate the stories. The collection of stories and poems (along with illustrations) can be compiled into a class book for future reference.

## Family activity

See "Making Beds" on page 106.

*Prepared by* Martha H. (Marty) Hopkins
*Edited by* William R. Speer *and* Daniel J. Brahier

Name _____

# Shapes Art

Many pieces of literature have illustrations that help tell the story. Below is a copy of a poem written by Shel Silverstein. Read the poem carefully and try to guess what his illustration looks like.

Shapes                                              My Illustration

A square was sitting quietly
Outside his rectangular shack
When a triangle came down—*kerplunk!*—
And struck him in the back.
"I must go to the hospital,"
Cried the wounded square,
So a passing rolling circle
Picked him up and took him there.

Write down why you think the illustration
in the book looks like yours.

_____

_____

_____

_____

_____

_____

"Shapes" is in a book titled *A Light in the Attic*. Look on page 77 to compare the illustration with yours.

How are they alike? _____

_____

How are they different? _____

_____

What part of the poem is missing in Silverstein's illustration? _____

_____

Why do you think he chose not to include it? _____

_____

From the *Arithmetic Teacher*, May 1993

# IDEAS

# Sorting SKITTLES/Graphing SKITTLES

## LEVELS K–3

### Background

When students are presented with colorful candies, a common reaction is for them to pick out their favorite colors. This tendency in explored in this activity, which focuses on organizing and displaying data, as well as exploring concepts of chance, by using a manipulative familiar to many students, SKITTLES bite-sized candies.

### Objective

To group, display, and interpret information by sorting and arranging data to construct "real" frequency graphs

### Directions

1. Before starting the activity, the teacher should purchase a large bag of snack-sized packages of SKITTLES in regular and tropical flavors. The teacher should also purchase five regular-sized bags of SKITTLES.

2. Make copies of the "Sorting SKITTLES" and "Graphing SKITTLES" activity sheets for individual and group activities.

3. Divide the class into small cooperative learning groups. Each group will receive a regular-sized bag of SKITTLES, and each individual student will receive a snack-sized bag.

   *a)* Have students guess the number of SKITTLES in their own bag and write down their guesses before opening the bags.

   *b)* Have students open their own bag and count the number of SKITTLES in it.

   *c)* Have students determine how close their guesses were.

*Prepared by* Karen S. Norwood *and*
   Yvonne M. Coston
*Edited by* William R. Speer *and* Daniel J.
   Brahier

4. Ask students to sort the candy by color using the activity sheet "Sorting SKITTLES."

   *a)* How many of each color do you have?

   *b)* How many SKITTLES are in your bag?

5. Using the activity sheet "Graphing SKITTLES," place the candy on the activity sheet to construct a pictograph, and then ask the students the following questions and have them write down their answers:

   *a)* Which colors occurred the most?

   *b)* Which colors occurred the least?

   *c)* Which number is larger—the number of green plus red SKITTLES or the number of yellow plus purple SKITTLES?

6. Have each student color in circles corresponding to the location of the candies on the graph using the "Graphing SKITTLES" activity sheet.

7. Give each group a regular-sized bag of SKITTLES and have them repeat items 4 and 5 using the regular-sized bag of SKITTLES and a copy of the "Graphing SKITTLES" and "Sorting SKITTLES" activity sheets.

8. Have the groups report their findings to the class.

9. Ask the students the following question: "Suppose someone else came along and saw your group-frequency graph. What could that person find out from these graphs?"

### Answers

Answers will vary.

### Applicable Standards

- **Communication**
- **Estimation**
- **Number Sense and Numeration**
- **Statistics and Probability**

### Extensions

1. Have students calculate class totals using a calculator.

2. Have students discuss and construct creative ways to display these data.

3. Have the students taste the SKITTLES and graph the results. Prepare a final report to be shared with the class.

4. Have students build towers of interconnecting cubes using one cube in the appropriate color for each candy. A small group of students might enjoy working on this project, using their frequency graphs as references.

5. Use the graphs to generate problems about numerical relationships.

6. Have students take a survey in another class or around the school about their favorite color of SKITTLES candy, and add this information to the final report.

7. Have each student write a few sentences about the most surprising or fascinating fact about their findings, and combine these sentences into a final report that can be displayed along with the graphs.

Name _____

# Graphing SKITTLES

Construct a pictograph for the number of each color of SKITTLES on the graph. Hint: let each circle represent one piece of SKITTLES candy.

| | purple | green | orange | red | yellow |
|---|---|---|---|---|---|
| 10 | ○ | ○ | ○ | ○ | ○ |
| 9 | ○ | ○ | ○ | ○ | ○ |
| 8 | ○ | ○ | ○ | ○ | ○ |
| 7 | ○ | ○ | ○ | ○ | ○ |
| 6 | ○ | ○ | ○ | ○ | ○ |
| 5 | ○ | ○ | ○ | ○ | ○ |
| 4 | ○ | ○ | ○ | ○ | ○ |
| 3 | ○ | ○ | ○ | ○ | ○ |
| 2 | ○ | ○ | ○ | ○ | ○ |
| 1 | ○ | ○ | ○ | ○ | ○ |

---

# Sorting SKITTLES

red _____

orange _____

purple _____

green _____

yellow _____

Total number
of SKITTLES
in the bag _____

From the *Arithmetic Teacher*, April 1993

27

# IDEAS

# Geometric Art

LEVELS K–2

## Background

Students in the primary grades tend to be at the visualization level of the van Hiele classification and either preschematic or schematic in their artistic thinking. Geometric shapes are viewed as total entities rather than composites of simpler parts. Students who think at this level believe that changing a figure's orientation in space, or on paper, changes its characteristics and it becomes a different figure. For example, they may think that a square becomes a diamond when it is turned 45 degrees but that it will become a square again if it is placed flat on one of its sides. Students at this level of thinking need opportunities to manipulate and construct geometric figures, identity a shape in a set of cutouts or within other shapes, and develop both standard and non-standard vocabulary (Crowley 1987).

## Objectives

To develop vocabulary related to spatial concepts; to recognize and manipulate basic geometric figures

## Directions

1. Discuss terms relating to position, such as *under*, *beside*, and *overlapping*. Some terms, such as *under*, may have more than one meaning. For example, *under* may mean that part of one figure is hidden beneath another or that one figure is located below another figure.

2. Provide each student with a copy of the "Geometric Art" activity sheet. The circular, rectangular, and triangular geometric shapes from the activity sheet must be colored with different colors, cut out, and placed in the frame following the teacher's directions.

3. Have the students create a design according to specific criteria such as "Make a picture so that (*a*) a square overlaps a circle, (*b*) a triangle is under a rectangle, and (*c*) something red touches something blue." Students may need to review these clues carefully so that all the conditions can be met. Prepare extra copies of the shapes for the students so that they can borrow pieces to complete the given requirements.

4. The completed "pictures" may appear quite different, since the criteria can be met in many ways. Discuss these differences and why they are or are not acceptable.

5. Have students finish their abstract work of art by placing the remaining pieces in a pleasing design.

6. Ask the students to explain the placement of the remaining pieces in a manner that describes the positional relationships; for example, "I put the big triangle on the circle."

7. Have students glue their designs on a piece of construction paper and display.

## Answers

Answers will vary. Be on the lookout for students who realize that squares are special rectangles. Understanding the rela-

tionship between squares and rectangles indicates that the geometric-thinking abilities of these students are more advanced than those of students who think rectangles must always have one set of sides that are longer than the other sides.

## Extensions

1. Use the activity again, but ask the students to create the criteria to be used to form the picture. Limit the number of shapes and colors that students can use.

2. Using cutout geometric shapes, students can create identifiable objects from their environments; for example, a rectangle and a circle can make a tree. They can also be given a specific task, such as, "Use the shapes to make a house."

## Reference

Crowley, Mary L. "The van Hiele Model of the Development of Geometric Thought." In *Learning and Teaching Geometry*, 1987 Yearbook of the National Council of Teachers of Mathematics, edited by Mary Montgomery Lindquist, pp. 1–16. Reston, Va.: National Council of Teachers of Mathematics, 1987.

*Prepared by* Virginia Usnick, Phyllis Knerl Miller, *and* Danna Stonecipher
*Edited by* William R. Speer *and* Daniel J. Brahier

Name _____

# Geometric Art

Make a picture so that a square overlaps a circle, a triangle is under a rectangle, and something red touches something blue.

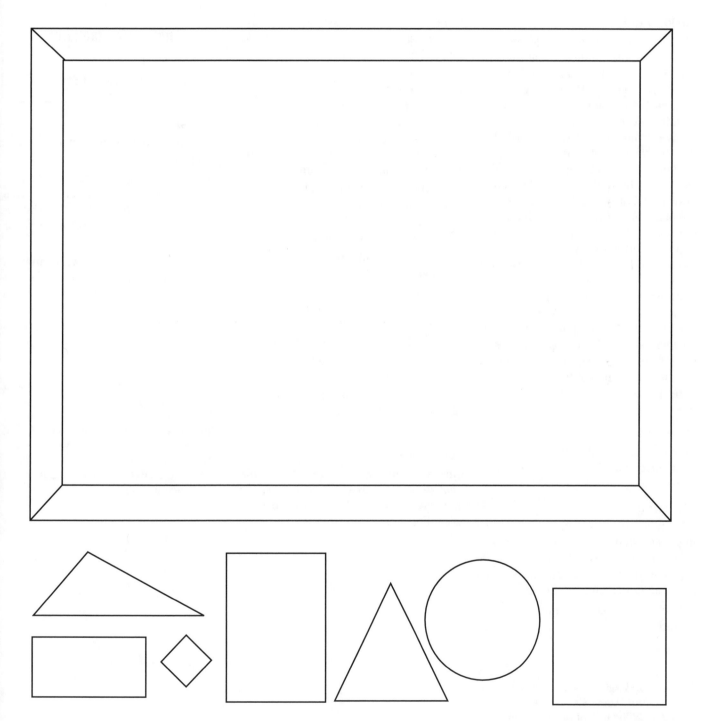

From the *Arithmetic Teacher*, March 1993

# IDEAS

# Shapely Art

## LEVELS 2–4

### Background

In the middle elementary grades, students' responses indicate that they are beginning to notice characteristics of geometric figures. They recognize figures as being made of parts and can identify the parts. Their thinking progresses from the visualization level to the analysis level. Artistically, more students are moving into the schematic stage. The natural way for children to draw in the preschematic and schematic stages is to put together geometric figures. In the preschematic stage, a typical child's drawing is made up of circles and lines. By the schematic stage, drawing has become more differentiated and elaborate but remains basically geometric. According to Crowley (1987), students at the analysis level should have opportunities to identify figures based on visual clues, identify properties of figures, and compare figures according to their properties.

### Objective

To locate and identify two-dimensional geometric figures on the basis of visual clues

### Directions

1. Supply rectangular patterns for tracing. Suggested sizes: 1 inch by 1 inch, 2 inches by 2 inches, 2 inches by 3 inches, 2 centimeters by 2 centimeters, and 3 centimeters by 5 centimeters.

2. Each student should choose only *one* pattern to trace.

3. Furnish a copy of the "Shapely Art" activity sheet, crayons, colored chalk, or markers to each student.

4. Discuss the term *overlapping* or demonstrate it by tracing a pattern on the chalkboard or overhead projector and reposition the pattern to overlap part of the original tracing. Color transparencies can also dramatically illustrate the result of overlapping.

5. Inside the frame, have students trace their chosen figure five to ten times, sliding and turning the pattern to overlap previously drawn figures.

6. Have the students locate any (*a*) squares and fill them in with yellow, (*b*) rectangles that are *not* squares and fill them in with red, and (*c*) triangles and fill them in with green.

7. Have students fill in other polygons with blue, while leaving the background white.

8. Have students cut out their framed abstract art and post it on a bulletin board.

### Answers

Answers will vary. Be sure the students realize that squares and rectangles do not have to be in the traditional horizontal orientation.

*Prepared by* Virginia Usnick, Phyllis Knerl Miller, *and* Danna Stonecipher
*Edited by* William R. Speer *and* Daniel J. Brahier

### Applicable Standards

- **Reasoning**
- **Geometry and Spatial Sense**

### Extensions

1. Use the activity again, but avoid making squares.

2. Use the activity again using two patterns that might be of different figures or of the same figure but differing in size. Consider using trapezoids or rhombuses.

3. Provide the students with tangram sets. Ask them to select two pieces that form a square. What pieces can be used to form a nonsquare rectangle? What is the greatest number of tangram pieces that can be used to form a rectangle?

### Reference

Crowley, Mary L. "The van Hiele Model of the Development of Geometric Thought." In *Learning and Teaching Geometry*, 1987 Yearbook of the National Council of Teachers of Mathematics, edited by Mary Montgomery Lindquist, pp. 1–16. Reston, Va.: National Council of Teachers of Mathematics, 1987.

Name _____

# Shapely Art

How many squares do you have? _____

How many rectangles that are not squares are pictured? _____

What figures have been made that are not rectangles? _____

_____

_____

From the *Arithmetic Teacher*, March 1993

# IDEAS

# Picturing Our Building

## LEVELS K–2

### Objectives

To analyze by sorting and classifying; to make conjectures and generalizations

### Materials

• A copy of the activity sheet for each pair of students

• Drinking straws or uncooked spaghetti to be used as supports, approximately forty pieces per student

• Pipe cleaners or modeling paste to be used as joiners, at least one-half stick per student (pipe cleaners cut to 1 1/2 inches long can serve as supports for straws; modeling paste is best if you use spaghetti)

• A large piece of brown paper on which to sketch landmarks

• Paints or markers

### Directions

1. Before the session, decide how to make the straws and joiners available to groups of students. You may wish to store them in dishpans or similar containers.

2. Ask students to take five straws and some modeling paste. Have them experiment with fitting two straws together. Then challenge students: Who can build the tallest free-standing structure with only nine straws? As students try to build tall structures, focus their attention on finding ways of joining straws.

3. After most students have finished, talk about tall structures, short ones, and some that didn't work. Did anyone have a tower collapse? Why did it collapse? How are the tallest structures made? Introduce some new vocabulary into the conversation here—refer to the straws as *supports* and the modeling paste as *joints*.

4. When your students can join straws and joints with some skill, focus on

*Prepared by* Rebecca B. Corwin
*Edited by* Daniel J. Brahier *and* William R. Speer

building a city or town. Ask them to close their eyes and think about the buildings they see when they are on the way to school or to the store. Take three or four names of kinds of buildtngs and record those on the chalkboard. Be sure you get different types and shapes. Encourage various answers. How are they alike? How are they different?

5. Pair the students and distribute a copy of the activity sheet to each pair. Tell students that they will be building structures for a town they will all design and will be putting those buildings on the designated piece of brown paper. Refer to the list on the chalkboard. You may want to encourage pairs to select one type, or you may prefer to allow students to build and see what comes of it. Pairs can build one structure together unless this level of cooperation is too difficult. If each student in a pair builds a different structure, require that they talk together about each one and count joints and supports as a pair.

Many of the students' ideas will change as they build. Further, these buildings will not necessarily look like the ones with which students are familiar; because of the nature of the joints and straws, some buildings will be quite unusual. Enjoy the opportunity to question students about the imaginary inhabitants or users of the spaces.

6. Allow sufficient time for students to explore this construction problem. Some students may need extra time to complete their structures. As the buildings are finished, have students place them on the large butcher paper, embellishing the town plan as they wish by labeling the buildings, creating roads or other landscape features, and adding details.

7. Focus a group discussion on the ways in which students relate to their structures and their town. This discussion may include the following:

• What are the functional aspects of the town? What is this town like *as a whole?* Does it have the kinds of buildings we need? Do we have fire stations? (This question may be difficult for younger students, who tend to focus on their own buildings rather than on a collection of buildings.)

• What are the structural aspects of the construction? Compare and contrast construction of the buildings. Do some of the buildings seem strong? Weak? How are the strong and weak ones similar? Different? Do joints with lots of straws in them seem stronger? Weaker? How would they advise other students to construct a strong building?

### Extensions

*Comparing heights:* When the town has been completed, ask students to analyze some aspects of the town. Are most of the buildings tall? Short? Which are the tallest buildings? How much taller are they than other buildings? How many times taller is the tallest than the shortest building?

*Counting and comparing numbers:* Ask students to count the number of straws they used in their buildings. Which buildings used the most straws? How many straws did it use? Which building used the least straws? How many were used? What other comparisons can students make?

*Measuring:* Using Unifix or other counting cubes, ask students to measure from various buildings to their own to answer such questions as, "How far is it from your house to the fire station?" and "Do you go farther than Jennie to get to the food store?"

Name _____

# Picturing Our Building

Make a building out of supports and joiners.

1. What kind of building did you make? _____

2. Count the pieces you used to build it.

   How many supports were used? _____

   How many joiners were used? _____

3. Draw your building below.

From the *Arithmetic Teacher*, February 1993

# IDEAS

# Building with Newspaper Dowels

## LEVELS 3–4

### Directions

1. About a week before this session, ask students to bring newspaper to school. Sunday newspapers are ideal. During the two days before the session, make newspaper dowels with your students. To do an effective job, take one double page of newspaper, start to roll it in one corner, and roll it tightly on the diagonal to the opposite side.

One piece of cellophane tape on the point will hold the dowel together. Ask students to make at least ten dowels each, and store them in the classroom. This is a good opportunity to practice mental arithmetic: How many dowels will we have if each person makes ten? If each person makes twelve?

2. Ask students to place their desks and tables along the side of the room so that you have some space to build. Perhaps a playground or gymnasium would allow more freedom of movement. Divide your class into groups of three or four. Supply the prerolled newspaper dowels and one roll of cellophane or masking tape for each group of students.

3. Tell students that each group is an experimental design team and that they are going to build structures with the newspaper dowels. They may fasten the dowels together with tape or with staples reinforced by tape. Tape may not be used as a support for any part of the structure, nor may tape be used to attach a structure to a piece of classroom furniture. All structures must be freestanding.

4. If you are concerned that the task is too open ended, you can suggest that students make an environment for a newly discovered animal. The characteristics of the animal you select should

have design implications for their structures. For example, "A new animal has been discovered that has some very strange physical characteristics. It has a long neck like a giraffe but two short legs like a pigeon. Its tail is curled like a pig's, but it is as long as its body, which looks like that of an ostrich. It always keeps its horselike head just above the ground so that it can sniff the area for signs of enemies. It likes to walk both back and forth and around and around. Your group has been asked to design and build a structure out of newspaper dowels that can serve as a temporary home for the animal at the zoo."

5. Allow students time to build. They will have to do some "messing about" to learn how the dowels can best be combined. Encourage them to observe one another's work.

Some general principles will emerge. You may want to record principles on the chalkboard as students work. For example, students may accidentally bend the dowels in the center and note that the dowels then become structurally compromised. You might then record a warning to be careful about bumping and bending dowels.

6. When you come to an appropriate stopping place, ask the teams to sit by their structures and analyze and compare their structures. How many dowels did they use? Do the structures have common characteristics? Are some structures very different from others? How would they characterize those differences? Which are the tallest? Which are the widest? What figures can be seen within the structures? Do some figures predominate?

7. Observe different groups' building techniques. How are dowels joined? How many supports come together at joints? Which group has joined the most dowels at one spot? Might there

### Applicable Standards
- **Communication**
- **Number Sense and Numeration**
- **Geometry and Spatial Sense**

be limits to the number of dowels that can meet at one place? Did some groups find ways of bracing their structures? How did those techniques develop?

8. Look at the kinds of space these structures define. Can we sit inside any of them? How does it feel to be inside them? If you covered the suggested surfaces with newspaper "walls," how would the spaces feel?

9. Ask students to comment on the process of building these structures. Did they have something in mind from the start? Did their ideas evolve as they worked? How did the spaces take shape and grow? Did the group spend time talking about how best to support their structure? Did their process seem to be mostly trial and error? What would they change?

10. Ask the students which structures seem to be the most rigid. Patting the tops and joints tells a good deal about the rigidity of each structure. Which of the structures seem to be the strongest? Do the strong ones have anything in common? How could the strength of the structures be measured? As students conjecture about strength and rigidity, you may want to make suggestions to explore.

11. Finally, ask students to record information about their structures on the activity sheet. You may want to ask students to make larger drawings and record these designs in a class notebook. You can use these as a baseline for comparison as students develop greater building sophistication.

*Prepared by* Rebecca B. Corwin
*Edited by* Daniel J. Brahier *and* William R. Speer

Name _____

# Building with Newspaper Dowels

Your group has made a structure out of newspaper dowels. Together, make a record of that structure. First, count the parts of your structure and record that information here.

Number of dowels we used: _____

Number of joints we taped: _____

Draw your structure below:




Write about your structure.

_____

_____

_____

_____

From the *Arithmetic Teacher*, February 1993

# IDEAS

# Figuring in Football

## LEVELS K–1

### Background

Geometric figures are very much a part of our environment and help define the ways in which we view and interpret our world. Everywhere we look we see the influences of pattern, symmetry, and design. A football field has numerous figures that a young student can easily distinguish and others, which can be rotated or embedded, that may call on more challenging spatial skills.

### Objectives

To identify and visualize congruent and similar two-dimensional geometric figures; to recognize that rotations, translations, and reflections do not change geometric figures

### Directions

1. Reproduce a copy of the activity sheet for each student.

2. Discuss with the class the fact that geometric figures are common in the world in which we live. Sports often use items of both two- and three-dimensional shapes, from the equipment used, such as balls and nets, to the playing fields on which the sports take place. In particular, football fields often include many geometric figures.

3. Have each student locate the geometric figures in questions 1 through 3 on the activity sheet. Students might be asked to outline the figures with colored markers.

4. Have the students study the diagram of the football field to answer questions 4 through 6.

### Answers

Answers will vary. You may want to prepare a transparency (fig. 1) of the

football field and colored transparencies of the various figures to use in helping students visualize the position of the figures. Some of the answers that students might produce include the following:

1. A. The circle surrounds the words *Super Bowl*.
   B. Several such triangles appear in the end zones.
   C. Several diamonds are found in each end zone.
   D. The triangles shown are at the top and bottom of both end zones.
   E. Several such pairs of triangles are seen in each end zone.

2. A. The oval surrounds the football field.
   B. The outline of the entire football field is such a rectangle. (A football field is 120 yards by 53 1/3 yards.)
   C. Several such parallelograms are in both end zones.
   D. Several "thin" rectangles can be formed using the yard markers.
   E. Hexagons can be formed using the line segments in the end zones.

3. Each of the five figures given can be formed using the diagonal line segments in the end zone.

4. The largest rectangle is the outline of

the football field.

5. Several small rectangles can be formed using adjacent yard "lines."

6. The smallest triangles are formed in the end-zone areas.

### Extensions

1. Have students make the same type of drawings for different sports fields, such as those for baseball, soccer, basketball, and tennis.

2. Have students collect from newspapers and magazines information about the Super Bowl that includes references to geometry (e.g., "the 10-yard *line*" or "the two teams *squared* off").

3. The activity page can be enlarged, and the figures that students are asked to locate can be cut out. These cutouts can then be used as "figure finders" by placing them on the activity page and sliding, turning, or flipping them until they cover a congruent (or similar) figure on the field.

### Applicable Standards

- **Problem Solving**
- **Geometry and Spatial Sense**

*Prepared by* J. David Keller
*Edited by* Daniel J. Brahier *and* William R. Speer

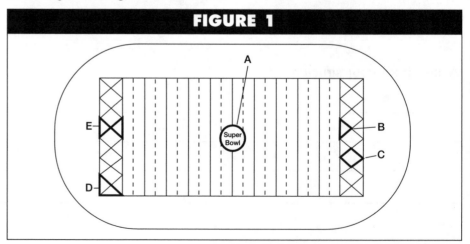

**FIGURE 1**

Name _____

# Figuring in Football

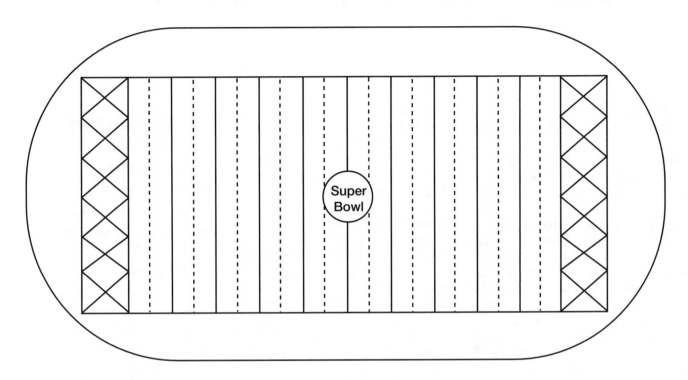

1. Find the figures on the football field that are just like these.

   A.      B.      C.      D.      E.

2. Find figures like these but of different sizes.

   A.      B.      C.      D.      E.

3. Find the figures that are just like these figures. You may have to rotate the figures to find the figure.

   A.      B.      C.      D.      E.

4. Find the largest rectangle.

5. Find the smallest rectangle.

6. Find the smallest triangle.

From the *Arithmetic Teacher*, January 1993

# Get the Picture—Get the Story

## LEVELS 2–4

### Background

Students frequently encounter problems or exercises that they are asked to "solve." In fact, in most classroom situations, the students *finish* problems rather than *solve* them. As teachers of mathematics, we are aware that students become better problem solvers when they are asked to take an active role in formulating some of their own problems. This activity page presents four pictures of things that students would typically find at a football game—players, a scoreboard, a crowd, and a concession stand. Students are asked to create problems that correspond to their interpretation of each of the pictures.

### Objective

To enhance problem-solving skills and emphasize mathematics as communication by creating and writing problems that represent given pictures

### Directions

1. Discuss with the students the idea that in many books, as well as in most testing situations, they have been given problems that they were asked to solve. Here they will also get a chance to become the problem writers. The students will become reporters at the Super Bowl. One job of a reporter is to write about what he or she sees. Explain that in this activity they will look at some pictures taken at the game and will write some problems to go along with what they see in the pictures.

2. Have the students work in pairs. Each student should be given a copy of the activity sheet. Explain to the class that for each of the four pictures, the pair of students is to create a problem and write it on the lines that accompany that picture.

Encourage the class to be creative in formulating their problems by not necessarily writing down the first and easiest problem that comes to mind. Also, encourage them to use a different operation, or an operation in a different way, for each picture. This restriction will help avoid having every group write a simple addition problem for each picture. This goal can also be accomplished by asking the students to write two different problems for each of the pictures as an optional activity, depending on the abilities of the class.

3. After everyone has finished writing four problems, have each pair of students get together with another pair (if even pairings do not result, then you may need to form one group of six) to share responses. Once the students have compared their problems, ask, "How many of you discovered that the other pair in your group wrote a problem for the picture that is different from yours?" Take this opportunity to discuss how a picture, a diagram, a graph, and the like are often perceived differently by different people.

4. As a conclusion to the activity, go around the room and have the students read their problems and count how many different types of problems were formulated from each picture.

### Answers

Answers will vary.

### Applicable Standards

- **Problem Solving**
- **Communication**
- **Connections**
- **Number Sense and Numeration**
- **Concepts of Whole-Number Operations**
- **Measurement**

### Extensions

1. After a Sunday of professional football games, clip from the newspaper the statistics from several games. Put each news clipping into an envelope with a sheet of paper and divide the class into teams of three or four students. Give each team an envelope. Their task is to write on the piece of paper one word problem based on the data in the news clipping, put the clipping and the piece of paper back into the envelope, and pass it on to the next team. The next team takes out the contents, solves the problem on the sheet of paper, and writes a new problem. That team then passes the envelope on to the next team. Continue this process until at least five questions have been written and solved for each clipping.

2. To connect art to mathematics, have each student draw a picture and write a problem about the picture. Then have the students exchange their drawings and have each student write a problem about the picture that he or she received. Finally, each student compares the problem that she or he wrote to the problem that the artist wrote originally to see if they are the same.

*Prepared by* J. David Keller
*Edited by* Daniel J. Brahier *and* William R. Speer

Name _____

# Get the Picture—Get the Story

You get to be a reporter at the Super Bowl! Reporters have to describe things that they see to their readers. Look at each of the pictures. What do you see? Write a problem about what the picture suggests to you.

_____

_____

_____

_____

_____

_____

_____

_____

From the *Arithmetic Teacher*, January 1993

# The Rhythm of Counting

LEVELS K–2

## Objective

To develop number sense through counting, including dividing a counting sequence into blocks of numbers. This exercise will eventually lead students into skip counting.

## Materials

- A tape recorder, a record player, a compact disc player, or some other device with which to play music
- Recorded music of your preference
- One instrument for each student: pair of wood blocks, drums, triangles, maracas, tambourines, pair of metal spoons, pot and wooden spoon, bells on pipe cleaners
- A copy of "The Rhythm of Counting" activity sheet for each student

## Directions

1. Listen to some simple recorded music of the teacher's choice. The following are music suggestions: Raffi songs and sing-song melodies, such as "London Bridge," "Pop Goes the Weasel," "Head, Shoulders, Knees, and Toes," "My Favorite Things," and "Are You Sleeping?" After listening to two or three songs, explain that each song has its own characteristic rhythm. Choose a song and have the students clap to the rhythm of the song as they perceive that rhythm. The students can also form a parade and march and clap at the same time.

2. Have the students sit down. Sing the song "Twinkle, Twinkle, Little Star" and have the students clap along to the music as you sing. Then have them sing along with the clapping. This activity helps students begin to hear the beat, or rhythm, of the music.

3. Next have the students replace the words of the song with numbers. Instead of singing "Twinkle, Twinkle, Little Star," the students should sing "one, two, three, four, one, two, three, four." That is, have the students count a number for each beat of the song, including rests. The line "Twinkle, twinkle, little star" takes two full four-counts, including the rest beat.

TWINKLE, TWINKLE, LITTLE STAR (REST)

1  2    3  4    1  2  3    4

HOW I WONDER WHAT YOU ARE (REST)

1  2  3  4    1    2    3    4

Students can clap along with this singing.

4. Repeat steps 2 and 3 with the song "Are You Sleeping?"—sing the song, clap, and replace the syllables and rest beats with the numbers one, two, three, and four.

5. Explain to the students, "We were able to sing the one, two, three, four over again because these songs seem to divide into groups of four. Let's try 'Are You Sleeping?' with the words *one, two, three, four, five*. How does this pattern sound? [Demonstrate the pattern.] Does this sound right? [We hope that students say no.] The song seems to divide nicely into groups of four but not so well into groups of five. Clapping four times per phrase seems to partition the song appropriately."

6. Next say to the class, "Let's 'sing' 'Twinkle, Twinkle, Little Star' by counting as high as we can to the tune of the song." (The class "sings" to 48.) *Note:* If students can count to only sixteen, or if the recitation to forty-eight gets too cumbersome, have them repeat "one, two, …, sixteen" three times. Be certain that the students recognize that the song still seems to separate into groups of four.

7. Direct the students to look at the activity sheet where the numerals 1, 2, 3, 4, …, 48 are found. Have them sing the song again as they did in step 6. Emphasize the rhythm by having students put a slash (/) after each of the groups of four beats.

8. Sing "My Bonnie Lies over the Ocean" with the class. Point out that this song is most easily divided into groups of three counts. Have the class

## Applicable Standards

- **Connections**
- **Number Sense and Numeration**
- **Patterns and Relationships**

sing the song by using the numbers one, two, and three instead of the words. *Note:* In this song, the word *My* is actually a three-count. The count the students need to complete is this:

MY BONNIE LIES OVER THE OCEAN MY....

3    1  2  3    1 2    3    1  2  3

9. Next, say to the class, "Let's 'sing' 'My Bonnie Lies over the Ocean' by counting as high as we can as we sing the song." (The class "sings" to 48.) *Note:* If the students can count to only twelve or if the recitation to forty-eight gets too cumbersome, have them repeat "one, two, …, twelve" four times. Be certain the students recognize that even though they used greater numbers, the song still seems to separate into groups of three.

10. Direct the students to look at the activity sheet where the numerals 1, 2, 3, 4, …, 48 are found beneath the lyrics to "My Bonnie Lies over the Ocean." Have them sing the song as they did in step 9. Emphasize the rhythm by having students put a slash after each group of three beats. Invite students to listen to some other songs that have three beats per measure. Clap out these songs and proceed through the activities in the same manner. Some good examples are "My Favorite Things," "Home on the Range," and "Chimchimcheree." Using the numbers 1–48 (or repetitions of 1–12), mark off the musical partitions.

11. Form an orchestra by dividing the class into three parts: the choir (singing the lyrics), the orchestra (using various instruments), and the conductors (counting the beat from 1 to 32).

*Prepared by* Barbara E. Moses *and* Linda Proudfit

*Edited by* Daniel J. Brahier *and* William R. Speer

# The Rhythm of Counting

Twinkle, twinkle, little star,
How I wonder what you are!
Up above the world so high,
Like a diamond in the sky.
Twinkle, twinkle, little star,
How I wonder what you are.

| 1 | 2 | 3 | 4 | 5 | 6 | 7 | 8 | 9 | 10 | 11 | 12 | 13 | 14 | 15 | 16 |
|---|---|---|---|---|---|---|---|---|----|----|----|----|----|----|----|
| 17 | 18 | 19 | 20 | 21 | 22 | 23 | 24 | 25 | 26 | 27 | 28 | 29 | 30 | 31 | 32 |
| 33 | 34 | 35 | 36 | 37 | 38 | 39 | 40 | 41 | 42 | 43 | 44 | 45 | 46 | 47 | 48 |

- - - - - - - - - - - - - - - - - - - - - - - - - - - - - - - - - - - - - - - - - - - - - - - - - - - - - - -

| 1 | 2 | 3 | 4 | 5 | 6 | 7 | 8 | 9 | 10 | 11 | 12 | 13 | 14 | 15 | 16 |
|---|---|---|---|---|---|---|---|---|----|----|----|----|----|----|----|
| 1 | 2 | 3 | 4 | 5 | 6 | 7 | 8 | 9 | 10 | 11 | 12 | 13 | 14 | 15 | 16 |
| 1 | 2 | 3 | 4 | 5 | 6 | 7 | 8 | 9 | 10 | 11 | 12 | 13 | 14 | 15 | 16 |

My Bonnie lies over the ocean,
My Bonnie lies over the sea,
My Bonnie lies over the ocean,
Oh, bring back my Bonnie to me.

| 1 | 2 | 3 | 4 | 5 | 6 | 7 | 8 | 9 | 10 | 11 | 12 |
|---|---|---|---|---|---|---|---|---|----|----|----|
| 13 | 14 | 15 | 16 | 17 | 18 | 19 | 20 | 21 | 22 | 23 | 24 |
| 25 | 26 | 27 | 28 | 29 | 30 | 31 | 32 | 33 | 34 | 35 | 36 |
| 37 | 38 | 39 | 40 | 41 | 42 | 43 | 44 | 45 | 46 | 47 | 48 |

- - - - - - - - - - - - - - - - - - - - - - - - - - - - - - - - - - - - - - - - - - - - - - - - - - - - - - -

| 1 | 2 | 3 | 4 | 5 | 6 | 7 | 8 | 9 | 10 | 11 | 12 |
|---|---|---|---|---|---|---|---|---|----|----|----|
| 1 | 2 | 3 | 4 | 5 | 6 | 7 | 8 | 9 | 10 | 11 | 12 |
| 1 | 2 | 3 | 4 | 5 | 6 | 7 | 8 | 9 | 10 | 11 | 12 |

From the *Arithmetic Teacher*, December 1992

# IDEAS

# Measuring Music

## LEVELS 3–4

### Background

Mathematical concepts are important in music. For example, the time signature is a pair of numbers whose lower number is some power of 2, typically 4, 8, or 16, and whose upper number shows the number of beats in a measure, most often 2, 3, 4, or 6. A time signature of 3/4 (read "three-four time") indicates that each measure has three beats, where one quarter note is one beat; a time signature of 4/4 (read "four-four time") indicates that each measure has four beats, where one quarter note receives one beat. The most common time signature is 4/4; 3/4 time indicates a waltz rhythm.

### Objective

To explore the equivalence of certain fractions and to give some examples

### Materials

• A copy of the "Measuring Music" activity sheet for each student

• A pair of scissors for each student

### Directions

1. Distribute the activity sheets. Have the students sing "It's a Small World." Ask such questions as these: Were all the notes held the same amount of time? (No) What is different in the appearance of the notes in the music that you see? (Some notes have stems; some notes are shaded; some notes are both shaded and stemmed.) Elicit comments that differentiate among all three types of notes in the music (quarter notes, half notes, and whole notes). What do these differences seem to mean in singing the tune? (They affect the amount of time a note is held; the notes without stems and without shading seem to be held for the longest amount of time.)

2. Sing the song again, clapping along with it. The students should be clapping on each beat; that is, for each measure,

*Prepared by* Barbara E. Moses *and* Linda Proudfit
*Edited by* Daniel J. Brahier *and* William R. Speer

they should clap four times. Explain, "Let's look at the notes in the last phrase (la, la, la, la). Sing only these notes and clap along. How many times did we clap? [4] How many times did we clap for the first note? [1] For the second note? [1] [Repeat this exercise for the first measure.] The music between any two vertical bars is called a *measure*." An example of a measure in the song "It's a Small World" is this:

3. Explain, "Let's look at the notes in the second complete measure. Sing these notes and clap along. How many times did you clap? [4] How many times did you clap for the first note? [2] For the second note? [1]".

4. Say, "Let's sing the last four measures and clap along. Look at the note in the second-to-last measure. How many claps did you give it? [4] What other types of notes could you have sung during these four claps? Let's do the following activity to find out."

5. Have students cut out the rectangles with notes that are pictured on the activity sheet.

6. Have students fill the rectangle labeled "one measure" with the cutouts from step 5. They should be able to identify six different combinations of notes that can make up one measure. (1 whole note, 2 half notes, 4 quarter notes, a half note followed by 2 quarter notes, 2 quarter notes followed by a half note, and a quarter note followed by a half note followed by a quarter note)

7. Have each student pick up a copy of the shaded note with a stem. Ask, "What part of a measure will this note's rectangle cover? [1/4] We can call this a *quarter note*." Instruct the students to pick up a copy of the unshaded note with a stem.

### Applicable Standards

• **Problem Solving**

• **Connections**

• **Measurement**

• **Fractions and Decimals**

Ask, "What part of the measure will this note's rectangle cover? [1/2] We can call this a *half note*." Ask, "What part of the measure is covered by the rectangle with this big circle? [The whole thing] Let's call this a *whole note*."

8. Explain, "We can put four quarter notes or two half notes or one whole note in a measure. So what part of the measure is one of these quarter notes? [1/4] What part of the measure are two of these quarter notes? [2/4] What part of the measure are three of these quarter notes? [3/4] What part of the measure is one of these half notes? [1/2]" Let the students explore the concept of equivalent fractions by observing the combinations of notes that constitute the same fraction of the measure. See how many equivalent fractions the students can discover.

### Extensions

1. Introduce the idea of eighth notes and repeat the foregoing activity with songs like "Old Dan Tucker" or "Are You Sleeping?" which are in four-four time and have eighth notes. Make a list of all possible equivalent fractions using eighths.

2. Select a song with a different time signature, such as six-eight time, and investigate what notes could make up a measure in this song. (Use a song like "Silent Night," "Sing, Sing, What Shall I Sing?" or "Pop Goes the Weasel.") List all possible combinations. Try to find equivalent fractions.

3. Have groups of three to five students create the words and beat (but not pitch) for a "song" using quarter notes, half notes, and whole notes in four-four time.

Name _____

# Measuring Music

1. Sing "It's a Small World."
2. Write numbers underneath each syllable for each time you clap.
3. Make a list of all possible sets of notes for which you can count four claps. _____

_____

4. What sets of pieces of a measure could be used to fill in the measure? _____

_____

5. What sets of pieces of a measure are equivalent to each other? _____

_____

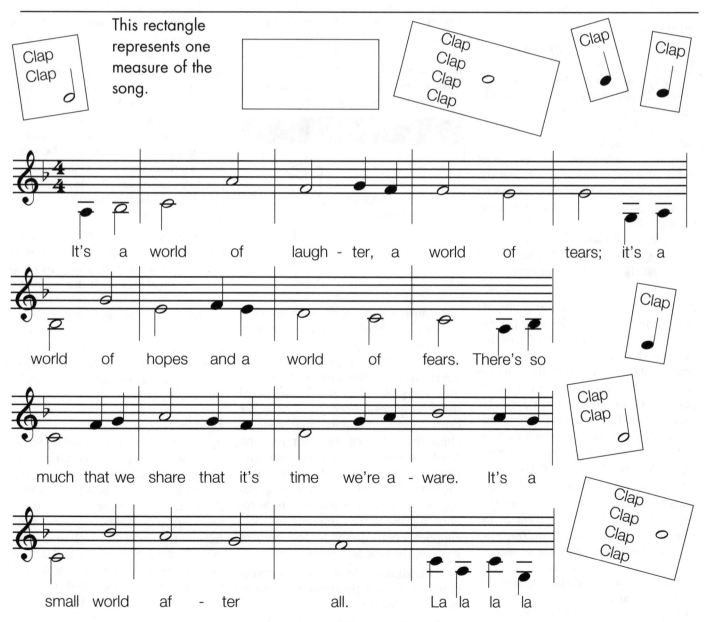

This rectangle represents one measure of the song.

From the *Arithmetic Teacher*, December 1992

# Which Flavor Wins the Taste Test?

## LEVELS K–2

### Objective

To conduct an experiment that requires students to gather and record data. Students represent the data by making a concrete bar graph and a picture graph, and then analyze the data. The activity also enhances counting skills as students gather the information.

### Directions

1. Begin a discussion by asking students to name their favorite cartoon character. Keep a list and a frequency count of their responses on the chalkboard. Point out that every person is unique and that not everyone likes the same things. Ask the class if they can think of any television commercials or radio advertisements that address the idea of a person's preferring one brand over another (e.g., students may respond that the two major cola manufacturers often claim that they are preferred over the others). Explain to the class that they will be conducting their own "taste test."

2. Out of sight of the students, prepare two pitchers of a powdered drink. For each pitcher, use a different flavor that can be distinguished by color (e.g., orange and lime). Label the pitchers "X" and "Y." Also prepare two *small* paper cups for each student and label them "X" and "Y." Making certain that the students do not see which flavor is in each lettered cup, pour a small quantity of each drink into the cups.

3. Put students in pairs. One student in each pair closes his or her eyes so that he or she cannot see the color of the drink or the letter on the cup. The other student gives the first one a taste of

*Prepared by* Daniel J. Brahier, Anne F. Brahier, *and* William R. Speer

*Edited by* Daniel J. Brahier *and* William R. Speer

each of the flavors in any order. Each student votes for the flavor he or she prefers and records its letter. Repeat the process with the students' roles reversed.

4. When the class has finished the taste test, each student brings to the front of the room the empty cup that had contained his or her preferred flavor. By placing a small piece of construction paper or cardboard between cups, students stack the cups with like letters to form a concrete graph of the results of the taste test, as shown in figure 1.

## FIGURE 1

A concrete graph of the results of the taste test

Because a large number of cups are physically difficult to stack, it is convenient to use an object to represent several cups. For example, if more than ten students choose a particular flavor, then every ten cups should be traded for a large can from juice or other drink. That is, if twenty-three students chose flavor X, then the concrete graph would consist of two stacked cans and three stacked cups, each marked with the letter $X$. Using a can in place of ten cups not only allows teachers to introduce representative graphing but also supplies a real context for the study of grouping by tens and place value.

5. Have students look at the concrete graph. Ask such processing questions as "Which drink was the favorite for the class?" "Do you think the results would

### Applicable Standards

• **Connections**

• **Whole-Number Operations**

• **Statistics and Probability**

be the same if another class did the same test?" "Why or why not?" "Would the results be exactly the same if we ran the experiment in this class a year from now?" "Why or why not?" "What do you think might happen if we added a third flavor to the taste test?" "How could we find out if the class liked another flavor better than the two flavors used in the taste test?" "Do television commercials that claim that people like one type of cola better than another necessarily mean that *you* will like it better, too?"

6. Using crayons or colored markers that match the drinks' colors, have students color in the cans and cups on the activity sheet to match the number of cans and cups in the stacks at the front of the room. The picture graphs now represent the results of the class's voting in the taste test. Have the class count the number of cans and cups in each stack and record that number on the activity sheet.

### Extension

Apply the activity to another subject area that is being discussed. For example, if students are studying the seasons of the year, they can be asked to vote for their favorite season and use a snowflake, a flower, a sun, and a fall-colored leaf with which to cast their vote. Discuss the results and ask students to explain their choices. In literature, students can be asked to vote for their favorite character in a story and explain why they chose that person.

Name _____

# Which Flavor Wins the Taste Test?

1. Color the picture graph below to match the cans and cups that you and your classmates stacked. Color one can for every ten votes given a flavor. Each cup stands for one vote.

 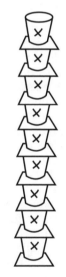  

2. Use the picture graph to fill in the table:

| Flavor of drink | Number of cans | Number of cups | Total of votes |
|---|---|---|---|
| X | _____ | _____ | _____ |
| Y | _____ | _____ | _____ |

3. Which flavor did the class like the most?_____

4. Which flavor did the class like least? _____

5. How many more votes did the favorite drink get than the second-choice drink?_____

From the *Arithmetic Teacher*, November 1992

45

# You Are the Pollster

## LEVELS 3–4

### Objective

To collect data, organize the data in a table, construct graphs of the information, and draw conclusions based on the information. Students can also determine the specific methods they will use to carry out the polls in the school.

### Directions

1. Put students in teams of two to four students each. If the school already has an eagle, pirate, or tiger as its mascot, the teacher will need to choose a substitute arbitrarily and replace the real mascot's name with that of the substitute on the activity page prior to duplicating the sheet. Distribute a copy of the activity sheet to, and secure a calculator for, each student.

2. Read the introduction on the activity sheet with the class. Explain that the first step in choosing the school mascot is to find out which mascot the students in your class prefer. Therefore, each student will vote for her or his favorite. When the voting has been completed, ask for a show of hands for each mascot and have students record the total votes in the table on their sheet. Students should then draw a bar graph of the results of the voting and answer question 3 on the activity sheet.

3. Discuss the responses to question 3. Students should be made aware that the top choice in their class may not be the most popular choice for the entire school. The classroom vote gave the students some information but not enough on which to make an informed decision.

4. Ask the class what they could do to get a better idea of how the entire school feels about the choice of mascot. Ideally, a student will suggest that an election be conducted for the entire school. This response will give teachers a springboard for explaining that the time is not sufficient to run such an election, since the decision needs to be made within one day. Explain opinion polls to the students. Around the time of an election, the news media frequently report data from such polls, such as "candidate A has a popularity rating of 30 percent." Teachers may want to refer to the preceding K–2 activity in which students conduct a taste test similar to those conducted for leading colas.

5. Explain to the students that they will be conducting an opinion poll to get a better idea of the entire school's opinion about the choice of a new mascot. Ask the class for ideas about conducting the poll, including the number of students to survey and its timing. The activity sheet is designed to allow each student to collect up to five responses for the poll. If the class thinks that each student should ask for more than five opinions, teachers should produce a second copy of the activity sheet for each student to record the data. Students will probably choose to collect the data in the lunchroom or on the playground. Have them collect these data on the activity sheet and bring it to class either later the same day or on the next class day.

6. On the chalkboard or the overhead projector make a chart like that in figure 1. Ask students to come to the chalkboard or the overhead projector and enter in the table the totals for each choice from their individual poll. With a calculator, total the responses for each mascot and record the totals on the activity sheets. Students should also draw a graph of the data.

7. The final step in the selection process is to discuss the data on the activity sheet. Processing questions might include the following: Was the class's winning mascot the same as the winner of the poll? Explain why or why not. Do you think the results would be the same if every student in the school voted for a mascot? Why or why not? Given all the information that you now have, what is the class's final recommendation for a mascot? Explain how you made that recommendation.

8. To summarize the activity, explain to the class that a poll is merely an attempt to get a sense of the voters and that it does not include everyone's opinion. Accurate results depend on asking as many different categories of people as possible and avoiding asking the same people more than once. For example, if no one in your class asked a fifth grader for an opinion, the information gathered may be inaccurate. For this reason, citizens should use caution and be somewhat skeptical of the results of polls.

*Prepared by* Daniel J. Brahier, Anne F. Brahier, *and* William R. Speer
*Edited by* Daniel J. Brahier *and* William R. Speer

### Applicable Standards

- **Problem Solving**
- **Communication**
- **Connections**
- **Statistics and Probability**

## FIGURE 1

| | Number of Votes |
|---|---|
| Eagles | |
| Pirates | |
| Tigers | |

Name _____

# You Are the Pollster

The students in your school have decided to choose a new mascot. The student council would like to use one of these: an eagle, a pirate, or a tiger. But they can't decide which mascot is the best. They have put your class in charge of choosing the best mascot for the school. You have one day to make the choice. The student council is depending on you to make the choice that makes the most people happy. The activities on this page will help your class make the decision. Good luck!

1. The first step is for your class to vote on their choice for a school mascot. Place an "X" in the box to vote for your favorite mascot.

 Eagles  Pirates  Tigers

2. Have students vote for their choice by raising their hands. Count the total number of people who voted for each of the three choices. Write the total number of votes for each in the chart. Then draw a bar graph showing the number of votes for each choice.

| Mascot | Number of votes |
|--------|-----------------|
| Eagles | _____ |
| Pirates | _____ |
| Tigers | _____ |

30
25
20
15
10
5

Eagles    Pirates    Tigers

3. Which choice is the most popular in your class? _____

Do you think this choice would be the most popular if you could ask every student in the school? _____

Explain. _____

4. Conduct a preference poll in your school about the choice of mascot. Record the results from your poll in the chart.

| Mascot | Grade 1 | 2 | 3 | 4 | 5 | Total |
|--------|---|---|---|---|---|-------|
| Eagles | ___ | ___ | ___ | ___ | ___ | ___ |
| Pirates | ___ | ___ | ___ | ___ | ___ | ___ |
| Tigers | ___ | ___ | ___ | ___ | ___ | ___ |

5. Add all the votes that you and your classmates recorded in the poll. Record these totals in the table and draw a bar graph showing the totals of the vote.

| Mascot | Number of votes |
|--------|-----------------|
| Eagles | _____ |
| Pirates | _____ |
| Tigers | _____ |

125
100
75
50
25

Eagles    Pirates    Tigers

6. What was the class's final recommendation for a mascot? _____

From the *Arithmetic Teacher*, November 1992

# IDEAS

# Exploring a Community

## LEVELS K–2

### Background

In this activity the students use mapping skills by locating various places and measuring distances on a map. Given the necessary data, they determine and compare the distances of several short trips. They also review some basic characteristics of common figures as they describe their location on a community map.

### Objective

To apply map-interpretation and compass skills as tools for analyzing and comparing information

### Directions

1. Prepare an overhead transparency of the map "Exploring a Community" on the activity sheet. Introduce the map to the students and have them identify the various buildings and places that are represented.

2. As you name each location on the map, have the students find it. Then have them brainstorm the functions and importance of each site. Discuss with the class such questions as the following: Which building is in the shape of a circle? Which two buildings have the same shape? Are they also the same size? In what shape is the park? How is the shape of the fire station like the shape of the police station? How is it different?

3. Introduce the compass rose and the directions north, south, east, and west as they relate to the rose. That is, on a map, north is always toward the top of the page, east is always to the right,

*Prepared by* Martha H. (Marty) Hopkins *and* Diane M. Gard
*Edited by* Daniel J. Brahier *and* William R. Speer

south is to the bottom of the page, and west is toward the left.

4. Use a simple diagram drawn on the chalkboard or overhead projector to discuss the directions of the compass. For example, convert figure 1 into a transparency. If we consider this transparency to be a simple map, which animal is south of the duck? Which animal is west of the fish? Which is east of the cat? Which is north of the dog? If students have undue difficulty, make a transparency of the compass rose from the activity and place it on the animal transparency so that the intersection of the compass rose's arrows sits on top of the animal in question. Doing so should help the students identify the correct direction.

5. Return to the "Exploring a Community" map. Practice identification of compass directions by asking questions and discussing the responses as a class, for example, What building is directly north of the library? What buildings are east of the park? What is north of the school? Describe the location of the empty lot on the map.

### Answers

The answers depend on the specific questions asked and the direction in which the discussion of these answers takes the class.

### Extensions

1. To assess students' familiarity with the names of various figures and their characteristics, have students color the areas on their map according to such directions as "Color the interior of the triangle green; color the buildings with four sides red; color the interior of the circle blue."

### Applicable Standards
- **Problem Solving**
- **Connections**
- **Geometry and Spatial Sense**

2. Ask the students to explore simple distances on the map. For example, what building is the farthest from the park? Have the students measure on the map with a piece of string to verify that the library is farther than the fire station.

3. Other questions that can be asked include "If I leave the school and walk north and east, what building will I reach first?" and "If I start at the library, in what directions would I have to go to get to the park?"

4. Have students play "Where Did I Begin?" Divide students into pairs. Have one partner secretly choose two places on the map—a starting point and a final destination. Direct that student to tell his or her partner the destination. From clues given about the routes leading from the starting point to the destination, have the second player guess the starting point. Then have partners switch roles and play

### FIGURE 1

48

Name _____

# Exploring a Community

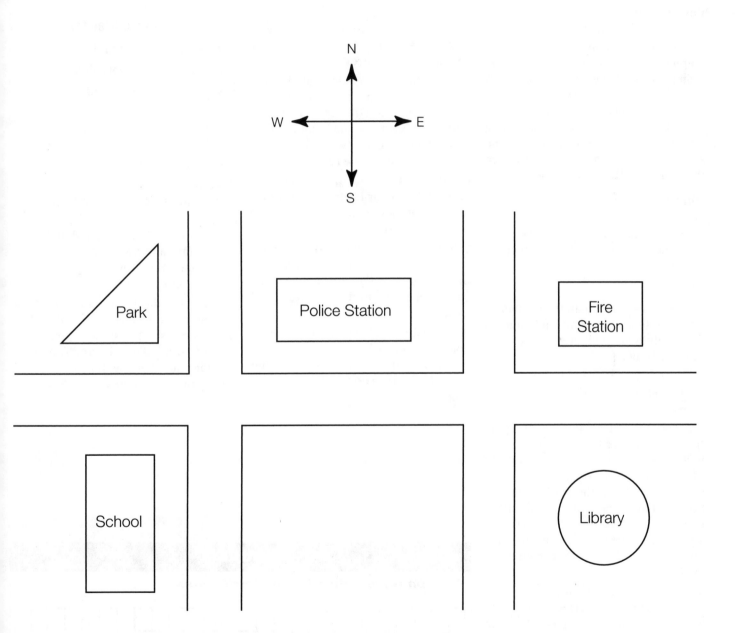

From the *Arithmetic Teacher*, October 1992

# IDEAS

# Getting to Know You

## LEVELS K–2

### Background

This series of activities gives students experiences in counting, comparing, graphing, patterns, and relationships. Using the first names and certain preferences of the students in the class and topics with which students are familiar from home or last year's schooling affords an excellent opportunity for the students to introduce or reintroduce themselves to their classmates.

### Objective

To explore number sense, number relations, and data analysis through activities that require counting, comparing, and graphing

### Directions

1. Students should count the number of letters in their first name and then listen carefully as each student says her or his first name.

2. Reproduce a "Getting to Know You" activity sheet for each student in the class.

3. Assist the students in completing the "personal ID card." First, have them write their name on the blank side of the card (if necessary, have the names already written on the card for them). Second, have them color around their name with a favorite color of crayon. Third, have them draw a picture of a favorite animal or pet beneath their name.

4. Assist the students in carefully cutting out the personal ID card. It should be folded so that the name-and-animal section and the alphabet section can be

glued back to back. Holes should be punched at the circles and then yarn threaded so that the personal ID card can be worn as a necklace.

5. Individual students should circulate among small groups or in the class as a whole to find another student whose first name has the same number of letters. Students can also find someone with one more, or one fewer, letter.

6. Students can group themselves according to their favorite color or the animal that they chose to draw on their personal ID card.

7. Students can be asked to stand so as to form a pattern from the information on the personal ID card, for instance, yellow, blue, yellow, blue or Ann, Brad, Consuello, Dimitri, ....

8. Compare students' preferences of color or animal by lining up the students behind a marker representing their choice, thus creating a human bar graph.

### Applicable Standards

- **Number Sense and Numeration**
- **Statistics and Probability**
- **Patterns and Relationships**

### Answers

Answers will vary.

### Extensions

1. Use the alphabet side of the personal ID card to create a graph displaying the number of each letter found in the students' first and last names. For example, Bobby Harris would draw a graph like that in figure 1.

2. Transfer the information from the human graph formed in activity 8 to a graph consisting of students' nametags pinned to a bulletin board. This information can then be transferred to a more traditional paper bar graph.

---

*Prepared by* Daniel J. Brahier, Shirley Hodapp, Rebecca Martin, *and* William R. Speer
*Edited by* William R. Speer

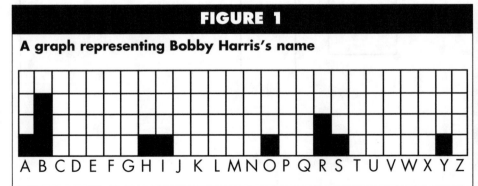

## FIGURE 1

**A graph representing Bobby Harris's name**

A B C D E F G H I J K L M N O P Q R S T U V W X Y Z

# Getting to Know You

fold

Personal ID Card

A B C D E F G H I J K L M N O P Q R S T U V W X Y Z

Name _____

Animal

From the *Arithmetic Teacher*, September 1992

# Have a Seat

## LEVELS 3–4

### Background

This series of activities involves students in number patterns, number sense, measurement, geometry, and graphing as they explore various seating arrangements in the classroom. Problem solving and the opportunity to share individual and group methods and solutions are parts of this experience.

### Objective

To explore the connection between numerical and geometric patterning

### Directions

1. Discuss the decision-making process that a teacher must go through when planning a seating arrangement for the class. Be certain that students are aware of such factors as the need for safe pathways between desks or groups of desks and the doors and walls. Also reinforce that desks can be arranged in many more ways than straight rows.

2. Reproduce a copy of the "Have a Seat" activity sheet for each student.

3. Pair students to generate and facilitate the discussion of questions.

4. Secure twenty-four square tiles for each pair of students. If necessary, these manipulatives can be made from poster board or index cards cut as 3-cm squares.

### Answers

1. $4 \times 6$, $6 \times 4$, $3 \times 8$, $8 \times 3$, $2 \times 12$, $12 \times 2$, $1 \times 24$, and $24 \times 1$. The answer regard-

*Prepared by* Daniel J. Brahier, Shirley Hodapp, Rebecca Martin, *and* William R. Speer
*Edited by* William R. Speer

ing preference will vary; however, discuss the reasonableness of having twenty-four desks in a single row.

2. The next triangle arrangement would require four more desks, as shown in figure 1. This pattern cannot be continued using exactly twenty-four desks. The sequence that describes this pattern is 1, 3, 6, 10, 15, 21, 28, ..., $n(n + 1)/2$.

3. Students may fill the grid but not limit the desks to twenty-four. Be certain that students leave space around each desk or group of desks as specified on the activity sheet. The grid for Mr. Hernandez's room should look as shown in figure 2.

4. Ms. Jofrans's room consists of twelve pairs of students, arranged as shown in figure 3. Less space is required to arrange the desks in this manner. When comparing the space needed for each arrangement, consider only the por-

tions of the grid that are necessary to complete the pattern.

5. Mrs. Beluso's room consists of six teams of four students. One such arrangement is illustrated in figure 4. Other arrangements that respect the requirements are possible. Any of the various groupings of foursomes, however, requires less space than arrangements of either single desks or pairs of desks.

### Applicable Standards
- **Problem Solving**
- **Communication**
- **Connections**
- **Number Sense and Numeration**
- **Geometry and Spatial Sense**
- **Patterns and Relationships**

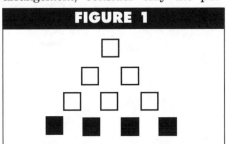

FIGURE 1

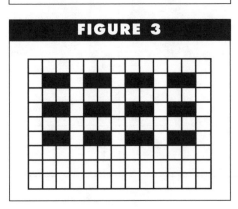

FIGURE 3

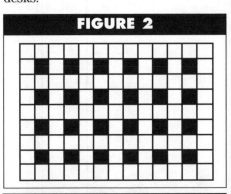

FIGURE 2

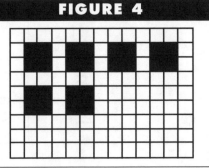

FIGURE 4

Name_____

# Have a Seat

1. On the first day of school, you find that twenty-four desks are in your classroom. One possible arrangement of the desks is four rows with six desks in each row, as shown. With your square tiles, find all possible arrangements of equal rows. Make a drawing of each below.

Which of these arrangements do you think would be best for desks in a classroom?_____

_____

Why would a teacher choose one arrangement over another? _____

_____

2. If a classroom had exactly three desks, they could be arranged into a triangle, as shown. If three more desks were added, another row could be formed to continue the pattern, as shown. How many desks would be needed to continue the pattern by adding another row to the triangle? ____ Draw a picture to show your answer.

Can the twenty-four desks be formed into a triangle following this pattern? ____ Show why or why not with a picture.

Three teachers, each with twenty-four students, decided to arrange the twenty-four desks in their classrooms in three different ways. They all agreed that the distance in front of, behind, and beside each desk or group of desks should be of at least the same size as a desk itself.

3. Mr. Hernandez decided to have each student sit alone with all the desks separated and began shading a grid to show how the desks would be

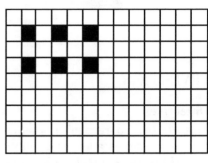

arranged. Finish the picture of the classroom by shading the remaining desks.

4. Ms. Jofrans wanted to put her students in pairs, so she began to sketch a picture of her floor plan. Finish her picture following the pattern she used. How many pairs of students were formed? ____ If we pair the students, do we need less space to fit all the desks in the room? Explain your answer._____

_____

_____

_____

5. Mrs. Beluso chose to make teams of four students. She didn't have the time to draw a picture like the other teachers. Complete one for her. How many teams of four students were formed?_____ Does arranging the desks in this way save more space than either Mr. Hernandez's or Ms. Jofrans's method? _____Explain.

_____

_____

_____

From the *Arithmetic Teacher*, September 1992

IDEAS

# Computation Court: You Be the Judge

## LEVELS K–3

### Objectives

*Case 1:* (*a*) To recognize whether a situation requires addition or subtraction; (*b*) to solve a real-world problem involving the subtraction of two-digit numbers

*Case 2:* To determine the value of a set of coins (dimes, nickels, and pennies)

*Case 3:* To solve a missing-addend subtraction problem

### Materials

*Case 1:* Set of coins: at least ten dimes, ten nickels, and ten pennies for each student or small group of students

*Case 2:* Set of coins: three dimes, one nickel, and two pennies for each student or small group of students

*Case 3:* Balance with gram weights

### Directions

1. Discuss the role of a judge in deciding a court case, emphasizing the need to justify the decision. Tell students that in "computation court," problem solutions are judged correct or incorrect.

2. Reproduce a copy of the activity sheet for each student.

3. Distribute the materials. Read each problem and its solution aloud. Encourage students to decide the verdict individually, using the materials as necessary.

4. After the students have made a decision, ask them to write the reason for their decision.

5. Because the students' reasoning may vary greatly, encourage them to share their answers with other members of the class.

### Important questions

1. Are the answers reasonable?

2. Are key words always helpful?

3. Can you find other, perhaps better, ways to solve the problems, especially for case 2?

### Extensions

1. Discuss and demonstrate possible solution strategies that could be used for each problem.

2. Prepare correct or incorrect solutions to problems found in the students' textbooks for them to analyze and discuss.

### Applicable Standards

- **Problem Solving**
- **Communication**
- **Reasoning**
- **Concepts of Whole-Number Operations**
- **Whole-Number Operations**

### Answers

*Case 1:* Julia's solution is incorrect.
*Case 2:* Melinda's solution is correct.
*Case 3:* Frankie's solution is incorrect.

*Prepared by* Martha H. (Marty) Hopkins
*Edited by* Francis (Skip) Fennell

# Computation Court: You Be the Judge

## Case 1

When Mrs. Jones came home from the store, she looked in her coin purse and saw that she had a total of 24 cents. She had 40 cents before she went shopping. How much did she spend altogether? Julia solved the problem like this:

I see the words *total* and *altogether*, so I know I need to add.

$$\begin{array}{r} 24 \\ +40 \\ \hline 64 \end{array}$$

Mrs. Jones spent 64 cents.

Verdict: ❑ Julia's solution is correct. ❑ Julia's solution is incorrect.

Explain how you know. _____

_____

## Case 2

Melinda had 1 nickel, 3 dimes, and 2 pennies. This is how she figured out how much money she had in all:

I have 1 nickel, so that's 5 cents. Each dime is 10 cents and I have 3 of them, so I have 30 cents in dimes. Each penny is 1 cent, so I have 2 cents in pennies. Altogether I have 5 cents + 30 cents + 2 cents. I have 37 cents.

Verdict: ❑ Melinda's solution is correct. ❑ Melinda's solution is incorrect.

Explain how you know. _____

_____

## Case 3

Frankie was given a "mystery box" and a balance with weights, as shown. He wanted to know how much the mystery box weighed.

This is how Frankie figured out how much the mystery box weighed:

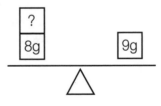

I need to find out what number I can add to 8 grams to get 9 grams. 8 and 9 are 17. The mystery box weighs 17 grams.

Verdict: ❑ Frankie's solution is correct. ❑ Frankie's solution is incorrect.

Explain how you know. _____

_____

From the *Arithmetic Teacher*, May 1992

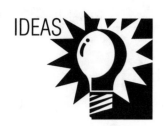

# Hop to It!

## LEVELS K–2

### Background
The students estimate the number of hops and jumps it takes them to cross the length of the classroom.

### Objective
To estimate by using nonstandard measurements

### Directions
1. Initiate a discussion with the students about the Olympic Games. Ask the students to tell you what they know about the Olympic Games. Record the students' ideas on a web similar to the one that has been drawn on the chalkboard. Discuss Olympic records with the students.

2. Distribute a "Hop to It!" activity sheet to each student.

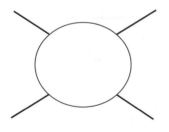

3. Ask the students to stand up and demonstrate a bunny hop (a hop with the feet together). Have the students look at the length of the classroom and estimate how many bunny hops are required to cross the length of the classroom. Have the students write their estimates in the box labeled "Bunny Hops."

4. Have the students hop in pairs across the length of the classroom and record the actual number of hops on the activity sheet.

5. Repeat the activity with frog jumps (jumps with hands and feet landing on the floor).

6. Ask the students to answer the questions on the activity sheet and discuss them. Ask the students if they can think of a way to move across the room that would take fewer steps than the frog jumps.

7. Elicit from the students that smaller jumps require a greater number of moves to cross the classroom.

### Applicable Standards
- **Communication**
- **Estimation**
- **Measurement**

### Extension
Hold other contests using such procedures as skipping, giant steps, and jumping rope.

### Answers
1, 2, 4, 5. Answers will vary.
3. Bunny hops

### Family activity
See "Olympics on the Home Front" on page 108.

---

*Prepared by* Kay B. Sammons *and* Beth Kobett
*Edited by* Francis (Skip) Fennell

Name_____

# Hop to It!

The Olympic Games are contests to find out who can run the fastest, jump the highest, and skate the best. Your class is going to have a special "olympics" jumping contest. The length of the classroom will be the distance for the contest.

1. How many bunny hops will you take to get across the classroom?
   Write your estimate and then try it!

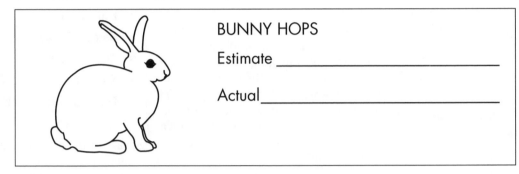

BUNNY HOPS

Estimate _____

Actual_____

2. How many frog jumps will you take to get across the classroom?
   Write your estimate and then try it!

FROG JUMPS

Estimate_____

Actual _____

3. Did you take more bunny hops or frog jumps to get across the classroom?_____
   Why? _____

   _____

4. How close were you to your estimates? _____

5. If you had to bunny hop the length of two classrooms, about how many bunny hops would you take? _____

   How do you know? _____

   _____

   _____

From the *Arithmetic Teacher*, April 1992

# IDEAS

# Long Leaps for Olympic Gold

## LEVELS 2–4

### Background

Students will estimate length, actually participate in jumping, measure the distance of a long jump, and compare the class's long jumps to Olympic records. Students will also interpret data from the table of long jumps and Olympic winning jumps.

### Objective

To estimate and measure length and compare and interpret data

### Directions

1. On a blank piece of paper, have the students draw a line segment about one foot in length.

2. Have the students show their "feet" to the class. Ask the students how they determined their estimate of the length of a foot.

3. Ask the students to measure their estimates and determine which ones are reasonable. Cut out the estimates and determine which is closest to a foot. Ask the students to estimate twenty feet.

4. Ask if anyone in the class could jump twenty feet. Tell the students that in 1896, the Olympic champion, Ellery Clark, jumped almost twenty-one feet.

5. Ask the students if anyone in the class could jump that far.

6. Have the students estimate how far they can jump.

7. Distribute the activity sheet to each student and have the students look at the Olympic long-jump data. Ask the students to describe the changes in the long-jump-record distances from 1896 to 1988. Have the students work in pairs to complete questions 1 through 5. Discuss the questions and answers with the students.

8. Take the students outdoors to jump and measure and record the length of their jumps. Mark off a line to show where the jump begins. Students may take a running start of any length. The jump is measured from the starting line to the nearest point of contact with the jumping surface.

### Extensions

1. Have the students research the current world record for the long jump. Mike Powell beat Bob Beamon's twenty-three-year-old long-jump record by jumping twenty-nine feet four and one-half inches in Tokyo at the World Track and Field Championships in the summer of 1991.

### Applicable Standards

- **Connections**
- **Estimation**
- **Number Sense and Numeration**
- **Measurement**
- **Statistics and Probability**
- **Fractions and Decimals**

2. Have the students explore the reasons that the Olympic Games were not held in certain years.

3. Have the students locate on a map the sites for the 1992 Olympic Games.

### Answers

1. About 8 feet, Bob Beamon from the United States

2–6, 8. Answers will vary.

7. Comparisons will vary.

9. Answers will vary. Answers between 28 and 29 feet are reasonable. (The actual distance was about 28 feet 5 1/2 inches.)

### Family Activity

See "Olympics on the Home Front" on page 108.

*Prepared by* Kay B. Sammons *and* Beth Kobett
*Edited by* Francis (Skip) Fennell

Name_____

# Long Leaps for Olympic Gold

The following are some of the winners of the Olympics long jump.

| Year | Winner | Country | Distance |
|------|--------|---------|----------|
| 1896 | Ellery Clark | U.S. | 20 ft. 10 in. |
| 1912 | Albert Gutterson | U.S. | 24 ft. 11 1/4 in. |
| 1936 | Jesse Owens | U.S. | 26 ft. 5 1/2 in. |
| 1964 | Lynn Davies | G.B. | 26 ft. 5 3/4 in. |
| 1968 | Bob Beamon | U.S. | 29 ft. 2 1/2 in. |
| 1980 | Lutz Dombrowski | E. Ger. | 28 ft. 1/4 in. |
| 1984 | Carl Lewis | U.S. | 28 ft. 1/4 in. |
| 1988 | Carl Lewis | U.S. | 28 ft. 7 1/4 in. |

Source: *The World Almanac and Book of Facts*, edited by Mark S. Hoffman (New York: Pharos Books, 1991)

Refer to the chart to answer the following questions.

1. About how many feet longer did Carl Lewis jump than Ellery Clark?_____

   Who had the longest jump? _____

2. Name some things that are about 30 feet long. _____

   _____

   _____

3. Is your classroom greater than, less than, or exactly 30 feet long? _____

   How do you know?_____

4. Estimate the length of your desk._____

   About how many desks would be required to make a row 30 feet long?_____

5. Estimate in feet how far you can jump long-jump style. About _____feet.

6. Find out how far you can jump long-jump style. Record the distance here. _____

7. Compare your distance with the 1968 Olympic record of 29 feet 2 1/2 inches. Compare your long-jump distance with those of your classmates.

8. About how many students' jumps would equal the length of Carl Lewis's 1988 winning jump?_____

9. How long do you think the winning long jump might have been in the 1992 Olympics?_____

From the *Arithmetic Teacher*, April 1992

# IDEAS

# Numbers on a Kite Tail

## LEVELS K–2

### Objective

The students place numbers on a kite tail to 100 and to 500.

### Materials

- A copy of the "Numbers on a Kite Tail" activity sheet for each student
- Scissors
- Glue

### Directions

1. Engage students in a conversation about flying kites. Ask them how high they think kites might go. Ask them how they might determine how much string they would need on their kite to let it fly very high in the air.

2. Tell the students that all the bows have fallen from the kite's tail and they will need to replace them on the tail where they belong.

3. Instruct the students to cut out the bows at the bottom of the activity sheet.

4. Have the students work in pairs to determine where to place the bows on the kite's tail and then glue the ribbons in place.

5. Have the students answer the questions at the bottom of the page.

6. Discuss with students their reasons for the placement of the bows on the kite's tail.

### Extensions

1. Cut a string about the length of the classroom. On index cards, write the numbers 0, 50, 100, 200, 500, or greater, depending on the students' ability.

2. Place the card with the 0 at one end of the string and the one with the 50 at the other end. Call out various numbers and ask the students to stand on the string to indicate where they think the number might be located on the string. Ask such questions as these: To which end are you closer? Why did you decide to stand there?

3. Ask a student to stand between two other students who are already standing on the string. Have the remaining students identify a number for that student's location.

4. Ask the students what will happen to the existing numbers if they change the endpoints. (If they change the endpoints to 0 and 200, then the location of the existing numbers changes. They will have to be moved closer to the 0 endpoint; for example, 87 would be placed near the 100 endpoint on the first string; however, changing the endpoints to 0 and 200 would cause 87 to be moved nearer to the middle of the string.)

5. Change the endpoints of the string to 1 and 500 or 200 and 500 and have the students place the numbers on the new string.

### Family activity

See "Number Sense at Home" on page 109.

*Prepared by* Kay B. Sammons *and* Beth Kobett
*Edited by* Francis (Skip) Fennell

# Numbers on a Kite Tail

Cut out the bows below for the kite's tail. Place them on the tail where you think they belong. Then answer the questions.

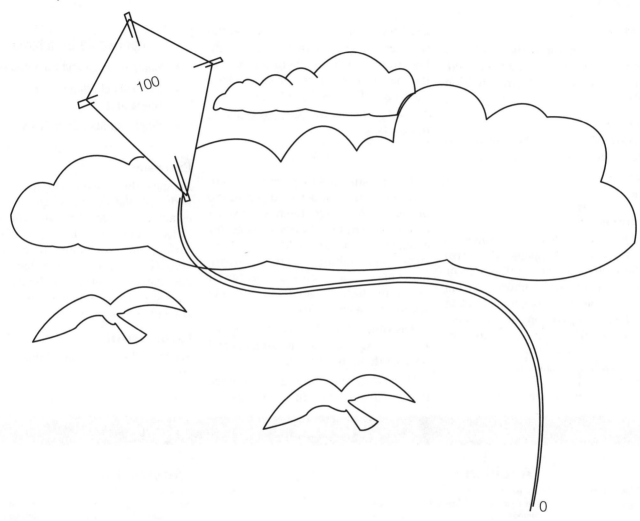

## Talk about It

1. How did you decide where to place the bows on the kite's tail?

2. Which bow is closest to 0? Closest to 100?

3. Which bows are between 0 and 50? Between 50 and 100?

4. Are any numbers on the bows greater than 80? How many?

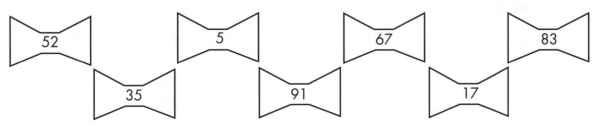

From the *Arithmetic Teacher*, March 1992

# IDEAS

# Pin the Tail on the Kite

## LEVELS 3–4

### Objective

The students determine the number of digits in the answers to addition, subtraction, multiplication, and division problems.

### Materials

- A copy of the "Pin the Tail on the Kite" activity sheet for each student
- Scissors
- Glue

### Directions

1. Engage the students in a conversation about what happens when two numbers are added, multiplied, or divided or when one is subtracted from the other. The students should explain the effect of operations on numbers (e.g., when whole numbers [except zero] are multiplied, the answer is the same as, or greater than, either number; when whole numbers are added, the answer is equal to, or larger than, the larger of the two numbers).

2. Display the the following example to the students:

$$27 \times 4 = \underline{\phantom{00}}$$

3. Ask the students to work in pairs to determine the number of digits in the product. Encourage them to use an estimation strategy to assist them; for example, a student could round 27 to 30 and then multiply by 4 to get an estimate of 120, a three-digit answer. If necessary, have the students complete several more examples.

4. Distribute the "Pin the Tail on the Kite" activity sheet to the students and instruct them to complete it.

5. Discuss the questions and encourage the students to share their strategies.

*Prepared by* Kay B. Sammons *and* Beth Kobett
*Edited by* Francis (Skip) Fennell

### Applicable Standards

- **Number Sense and Numeration**
- **Concepts of Whole-Number Operations**
- **Whole-Number Operations**

### Extension

Arrange the students in four groups with calculators. Each group should establish a range of answers for operations in addition, subtraction, multiplication, and division. Distribute an activity sheet on which have been duplicated the charts in figure 1 and have students complete them. Have the students share their results.

### Family activity

See "Number Sense at Home" on page 109.

---

## FIGURE 1

### Addition

| Number of digits in first number | Number of digits in second number | Smallest sum | Largest sum |
|---|---|---|---|
| 1 | 1 | | |
| 2 | 2 | | |
| 3 | 2 | | |
| 3 | 3 | | |
| 4 | 2 | | |

### Subtraction

| Number of digits in first number | Number of digits in second number | Smallest difference | Largest difference |
|---|---|---|---|
| 2 | 1 | | |
| 3 | 2 | | |
| 4 | 3 | | |
| 4 | 2 | | |
| 5 | 2 | | |

### Multiplication

| Number of digits in first number | Number of digits in second number | Smallest product | Largest product |
|---|---|---|---|
| 1 | 1 | | |
| 2 | 2 | | |
| 3 | 2 | | |
| 3 | 3 | | |
| 4 | 2 | | |

### Division

| Number of digits in dividend | Number of digits in divisor | Smallest quotient | Largest quotient |
|---|---|---|---|
| 2 | 1 | | |
| 2 | 2 | | |
| 3 | 1 | | |
| 3 | 2 | | |
| 4 | 2 | | |

IDEAS

Name_____

# Pin the Tail on the Kite

Look at the following kites. Notice that each kite is labeled for two-digit, three-digit, or four-digit numbers. At the bottom of the sheet are addition, subtraction, multiplication, and division problems on kite-tail bows. Cut out the bows and without computing, decide how many digits are in the answer to each problem. Then place the bow on the proper kite tail. On the blank bows, write your own problems and place them on the correct kite tail. Answer the questions below.

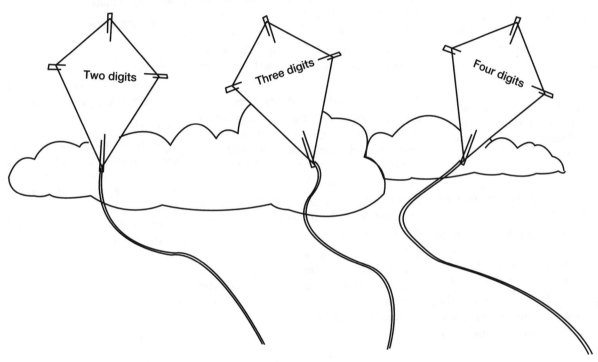

**Talk about It**

1. How did you decide where to place the bows?
2. Which bows were easier to place on the kite tail? Why?
3. Which bow was the hardest to place on the kite tail? Why?
4. How did you create the problems for the blank bows?

| | | | | |
|---|---|---|---|---|
| 99 + 17 | 23 × 2 | 1298 + 245 | 927 + 79 | 905 ÷ 3 |
| 105 − 22 | 159 ÷ 5 | 23 × 5 | 345 × 5 | 876 − 799 |

From the *Arithmetic Teacher*, March 1992

IDEAS

# How Big Is Your Heart?

## LEVELS K–2

### Background
This activity sheet focuses on the relative size of the heart. The activities relate the dimensions of the fist to those of the heart. Making predictions and models is an integral component of this activity.

### Objective
To measure the length, width, and circumference of the student's fist and relate these dimensions to the size of the heart

### Directions
1. Reproduce a copy of the activity sheet for each student.

2. Read the introductory information to the students and give each student or group of students a piece of string approximately 40 cm long and a ruler.

3. Have the students measure the length and width of their fist. Then ask them to wrap the string around their fist, including their thumb, and measure that distance with their ruler. Some students may ask what to do, since the thumb may protrude as they make their fist.

4. Based on their fist's length, have the students estimate the length of their heart.

5. Next have the students determine the distance around the fist of a teacher, an older friend, and a parent and complete the questions about the relative sizes of their elders' fists and respective hearts.

6. Have the students predict how long and wide their heart will be when they become sixteen years old.

7. Finally, have the students make models of their heart, using their fist as a guideline. Have the students record the length and width of, and distance around, their model.

### Applicable Standards
- **Connections**
- **Measurement**

### Answers
Answers will vary according to the sizes of the students' fists.

### Extension
Have students estimate the weight of a human heart (less than 1 lb.—about 0.5 kg) and then compare it with the weights of the following animals' hearts:

| | |
|---|---|
| Blue whale | 1000 lbs., or 450 kg |
| Gray whale | 300 lbs., or 135 kg |

*Prepared by* Lisa M. Passarello *and*
  Francis (Skip) Fennell

Name _____

# How Big Is Your Heart?

Your heart is a machine. It pumps blood to all parts of your body. The bigger the person, the bigger the heart. Your heart is about the size of your fist. Your heart and fist will grow at about the same rate.

1. Make a fist. Use string and a ruler to find—
   • its length: _____
   • its width: _____
   • the distance around your fist: _____

2. On the basis of the measurements you made, about how long do you think your heart is? _____

3. Find the distance around the fist of—
   • your teacher: _____
   • an older friend: _____
   • a parent: _____

Whose fist is biggest?

_____

Whose heart do you think
is the biggest?

_____

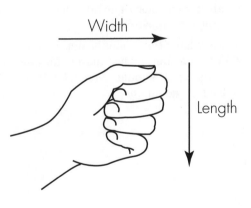

4. How long do you think your heart will be when you are sixteen years old? _____
   How wide? _____

5. Using your fist as a model, make a paper model of your heart. Write the distance around the model of your heart and its length and width.

From the *Arithmetic Teacher*, February 1992

# IDEAS

# Every Beat of Your Heart

## LEVELS 3–4

### Background

This activity involves taking a pulse, collecting and interpreting data, making predictions, and drawing conclusions. Its focus is the collection and analysis of data.

### Objective

To collect, organize, and interpret data, including making predictions, involving the heart rate at rest and after exercise

### Directions

1. Reproduce a copy of the activity sheet for each student.

2. Have the students read the introductory statement, which defines heart rate and explains how it is determined by taking the pulse.

3. Demonstrate how a pulse is taken. As the students work individually or in small groups, have them take their resting pulse for one minute.

4. Next have the students step up and down on a stair, or just march, for one minute. They should then take their pulse for one minute.

5. Have the same students determine their one-minute heart rates after running in place for one minute and after walking for one minute.

6. Have the students complete questions 1–5 and discuss the responses.

### Answers

Answers will vary. Make sure that the students can actually feel their pulse as they time it.

### Extensions

1. Record on a classroom chart the students' heart rates at rest and after the various forms of exercise. Discuss the class's range of heart rates at rest and after exercise.

2. Students may enjoy determining the heart rate of a favorite pet. Have them share their results with the class.

3. Students can use any of the following people for this experiment: yourself, a friend, an older person, a younger person, a parent, a teacher, your principal. They should have three people run in place for one minute and then count their heartbeats for one minute. Have students answer the following:

*a*) Which person had the most heartbeats? How many?

*b*) What range of heartbeats was recorded?

*c*) What conclusions can you draw from your experiment?

### Applicable Standards
- **Problem Solving**
- **Connections**
- **Number Sense and Numeration**
- **Statistics and Probability**

*Prepared by* Lisa M. Passarello *and* Francis (Skip) Fennell

IDEAS

# Every Beat of Your Heart

Name_____

The heart of a child below the age of twelve beats about 100 times a minute. Try the following experiment. Check your heartbeat by pressing your fingers as shown below to find your pulse. The pulse is the throbbing, or beating, felt when blood is pumped by the heart. Once you can feel your pulse, count how many times your heart beats in one minute. Determine the following:

Number of heartbeats in one minute while at rest:

_____

Number of heartbeats in one minute after exercise:

Stepping up and down        _____

Walking        _____

Running in place        _____

Inside of wrist

1. Does the heart beat faster at rest or after exercise? _____

2. Which exercise caused the heart to beat the fastest? _____

3. Would the heart beat faster if you exercised for more than one minute?_____
   Why?_____

4. Do you think the heart would beat faster after running or after biking?_____
   How could you test your prediction?_____

5. Whose heart would beat faster—a person who has just run a long race or someone who has just played a baseball game?_____ How could you find out?_____

From the *Arithmetic Teacher*, February 1992

IDEAS

# Discovering Figures

## LEVELS K–2

### Objectives

Students explore using geometric figures and make various patterns. They discover the attributes of each figure and use their pieces to design a square for a quilt.

### Materials

A six-inch-by-six-inch paper mat, cutouts of the patterns on the "Discovering Figures" activity sheet (students can cut out their own figures), glue, paper, scissors, a sticky-note pad, cards with the numbers 3, 4, and 6 written on them

### Vocabulary

*Pattern, square, rectangle, hexagon, trapezoid, triangle, circle, rhombus, gap*

### Directions

1. Place cutouts of pattern blocks in a learning center for free exploration at least one week prior to using them for instruction.

2. When the students are ready for direct instruction, give each of them one of each figure (circle, square, non-square rectangle, triangle, trapezoid, hexagon, two rhombuses). Discuss the various characteristics of each figure, for instance, the circle is round, the square has four angles, and so on. The simple game "I'm thinking of a figure" could be played at this time. The teacher says, "I'm thinking of a figure that has only three sides. Which figure am I thinking of?" The students then hold up the appropriate figure (triangle). The teacher can tell by looking around if the students understand the attribute of the figure.

3. Ask the students to look at the non-square rectangle and the square and tell what is alike in the figures (four sides, angles of the same size) and what is different (each pair of sides is of a different length on the rectangle). Have the students put the pieces side by side to discover the various characteristics.

4. Make a chart on the chalkboard or a large piece of paper and write two of the words, say, *circle* and *rectangle*, at the top. Ask the students to find an object in the classroom that has the same shape as either a circle or a rectangle. As they give the name of a circular or rectangular object, write it on the chart and give them one piece of paper from a sticky-note pad with the appropriate word on it. Have them place the paper on the object they have just identified.

Ask the students to select the trapezoid from the cutouts. Discuss how the trapezoid differs from the square and the rectangle. (All have four sides and four angles, but the trapezoid's angles aren't all of the same size.) Add the word *trapezoid* to the chart and find objects in the classroom that are shaped like trapezoids.

Have the students add the rhombuses to the set of figures and note that they also have four sides but that the opposite pairs of angles are of the same size. Discuss the shape of the rhombuses.

Repeat the foregoing procedures with the square, the triangle, and the hexagon.

5. Make a set of large cutouts, and clear off one small bulletin board to use to play the game "add a figure." Start the game by placing one shape in the middle of the bulletin board. The students complete the bulletin board. Each piece must touch but not cover another piece, and no gaps are allowed in the design. Explain what is meant by *gaps*. Each student draws one card from a stack of cards with the numbers 3, 4, and 6 written on them. These numbers represent the number of sides in the figure that the students are allowed to place on the bulletin board. For instance, those who draw a "3" can place a triangle, and those who draw a "6," a hexagon. As the students add a piece to the board, they must identify the figure, the number of sides, and the number of angles. After several pieces have been added, ask the students to predict which pieces will fit on the design. If students have pieces that will not fit immediately, have them hold them until they will fit.

6. Give each student a six-by-six mat and some cutouts. Have students place the cutouts on the mat as they did the large pieces on the bulletin board to create their own designs.

7. Give each student some glue and some figures cut from colored paper, with each figure available in a choice of several different colors. Have students create a design and glue it onto the mat. These "Designs of the Day" can replace the big design on the bulletin board.

8. Read to the students a story similar to *The Josefina Story Quilt* by Eleanor Coerr (New York: Harper & Row Junior Books Group, 1989). Explain the meaning of *quilt*. If possible, bring a quilt into the classroom. Discuss the various figures that are put together to make a large pattern, and tell the students that they are going to make a classroom quilt using the figures. Each student uses the figures to make one square of the quilt. The teacher then assembles all the squares onto a bulletin board or a large piece of chart paper to resemble a quilt, which is displayed in the classroom.

### Family activity

See "Patterns at Home" on page 111.

### Applicable Standards

• **Reasoning**

• **Connections**

• **Geometry and Spatial Sense**

# Discovering Figures

Figures for use as patterns in "Discovering Figures"

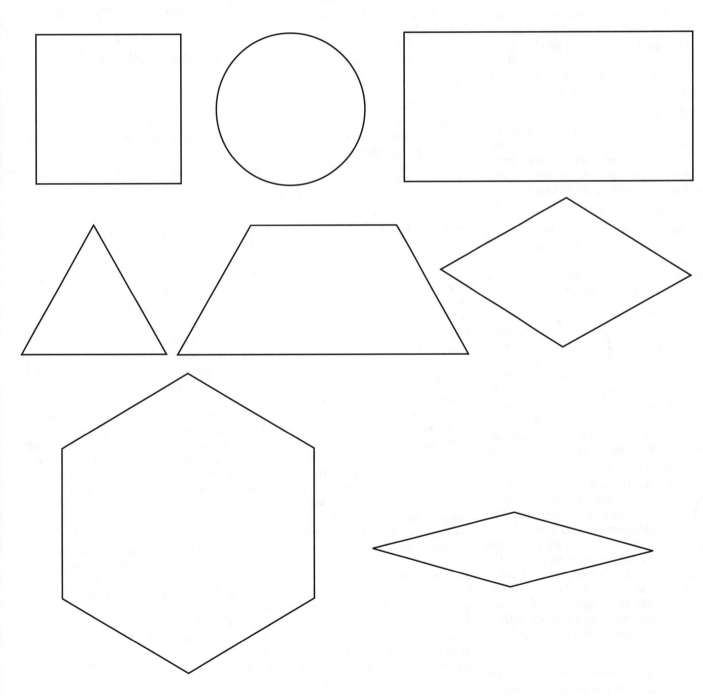

From the *Arithmetic Teacher,* January 1992

# IDEAS

# Geometric Figures

## LEVELS 3–4

### Objective

Through exploration, the students discover the attributes of figures appropriate for grades K–4. They predict which figures will cover a given area and justify their predictions by constructing patterns to cover the area.

### Materials

A copy of the "Geometric Figures" activity sheet for each student, pattern blocks for students who haven't previously used a three-dimensional model, mat papers, and colored cutouts

### Vocabulary

*Pattern, square, rectangle, triangle, rhombus, kite, circle, trapezoid, parallelogram, hexagon, tessellation,* and other words the teacher thinks the students do not understand

### Directions

1. To begin the work on patterning, show pictures of patterns. Follow with a discusion of patterning and what makes up a pattern. Look for patterns in the classroom and around the school. Ask such questions as, "How do we know that this arrangment is a pattern?" "Can we make our own patterns?" "What figures are used to make these patterns?" and so forth.

2. Distribute to each student a sheet of the geometric figures that have been photocopied from the "Geometric Figures" activity sheet onto construction paper or lightweight oaktag of various colors. Ask the students to cut out the figures, and give each an envelope in which to store them. Invite the students to exchange colors so that each has a complete set of shapes with at least two colors in the set.

3. After a period of exploration, ask the students to classify the figures in some manner, for example, by the number of sides, by the attributes of having sides or angles of the same size, and so on. Conduct a discussion of students' classifications.

4. Give the students a six-inch-by-six-inch mat and the "Geometric Figures" activity sheet. List on the chalkboard the students' predictions as to whether the figures tessellate. (Answer: All figures except the circle will cover the mat.) After all predictions have been made, have the students exchange figures so that each student has multiple copies of one of them. Each student should cover the mat with one figure. No gaps are permitted on the mat, and the figures cannot overlap each other; the figures can, however, extend off the side of the mat.

5. After each student has investigated a figure, verify the predictions. If a prediction cannot be verified, discuss the discrepancy with the class.

6. Give the students a set of figures and a mat. Ask them to construct their own patterns, using only the figures that they have discovered will tessellate the mat. Put the others aside for later use. Have the students glue their tessellation to the mat. Place the tessellations on a bulletin board labeled "Tessellations of the Day." Use the tessellations on the mats to help students discover the meaning of the word *tessellation.*

### Extensions

1. After the students have had a chance to develop their patterns, assign them to groups of two or three students who used the same figure. Give each of the students figures of a different color and ask them to combine them to make a new pattern. Teachers might want to use a large sheet of paper for this activity. Have students glue their figures onto the paper and display the designs in the classroom.

2. Have three students, each using a different figure, work together to make a pattern. The colors can be determined by either the students or the teacher. Again, students might use a larger sheet of paper on which to glue down their pattern. Display the patterns and discuss likenesses and differences in patterns.

3. Discuss the designs on Native American headbands. If possible, bring in some headbands or pictures of them. Help the students notice the various geometric figures used. After the students have discussed the designs, tell them they are going to make their own headbands using geometric figures. Give them several pieces of paper or three-inch-by-five-inch index cards. Have them make the same pattern on each piece of paper or card (they could glue small figures on the paper or draw the design with crayons). They will need to connect enough paper or cards to fit around their head. After the students have completed all the cards, punch holes in each card, tie the cards together with yarn, and wear them as Native American headbands.

### Family Activity

See "Patterns at Home" on page 111.

*Prepared by* Mary Lou Nevin
*Edited by* Francis (Skip) Fennell

### Applicable Standards

- **Problem Solving**
- **Geometry and Spatial Sense**
- **Patterns and Relationships**

Name_____

# Geometric Figures

| Name of figure | Number of sides | Number of angles | Will it tessellate (cover the mat)? |
|---|---|---|---|
| | | | |
| | | | |
| | | | |
| | | | |
| | | | |
| | | | |
| | | | |
| | | | |

Figures to photocopy for use in "Geometric Figures"

From the *Arithmetic Teacher*, January 1992

# Toy-Shop Numbers

### Background

A toy-shop theme is used to help stimulate and generate discussion about numbers. The examples on the activity sheet have been selected first to help students identify where they might find numbers in the real world. Second, students can use the ideas on the sheet or other ideas they have suggested in the discussion to write about numbers. Students will need paper and pencil to complete the activity.

### Objective

Students will be involved in discussing, describing, reading, and writing about one-, two-, and three-digit whole numbers.

### Directions

1. Reproduce a copy of the activity sheet for each student.

2. Generally discuss the toy-shop picture with the students. Ask them to tell what they see in the picture and what they think the picture is about. The students should name each of the objects in the picture. On the chalkboard, write the names of the objects as each is suggested.

3. Ask the students to look at the picture and find examples of the use of numbers. If more assistance is required, refer to each of the words on the chalkboard and have the students identify how numbers were used with each object.

4. Ask the students to tell some ways in which numbers might be used in a toy shop that are not shown in the picture. Allow enough time to discuss this question so all students have had a chance to offer a suggestion.

Some suggestions include—

• the prices on the toys,

• the number of ping-pong balls in the package, and

• the length of the jump rope.

Have the students write numbers on the activity sheet for the prices, numbers, lengths, and so on, that are suggested.

5. Read the directions at the bottom of the sheet with the class. The students can then work independently or in small groups to complete the activities. They should be encouraged to write descriptions of different ways in which numbers are used. First, have the students prepare a draft of their writing. Help them edit their work, correcting spelling, checking the use of capital letters, and suggesting appropriate sentence structure. Then have the students

### Applicable Standards
• **Communication**
• **Number Sense and Numeration**
• **Concepts of Whole-Number Operations**

copy a final version, for which they can illustrate what they wrote.

6. Ask some students to share the writing they completed for question 3.

### Extensions

1. Have the students work together to make a collage of information for another shop. They could work in small groups to make a manila-folder collage or as a whole class to make a bulletin board. Before they begin, the students should discuss various ways they might find numbers used in the shop.

2. Have each student select a favorite number. Make sure that the number chosen by each student is appropriate for his or her age. Each child should write reasons that the chosen number is a favorite.

### Family activity

See "Numbers at Home" on page 112.

*Prepared by* Calvin Irons *and* Rosemary Irons
*Edited by* Francis (Skip) Fennell

# Toy-Shop Numbers

1. Pick one number you see in the toy store.
2. Think how that number is used.
3. On the other side of this sheet, write a story to tell how that number is used.
4. Tell your story to the class.

From the *Arithmetic Teacher*, December 1991

# Post-Office Numbers

## LEVELS 3–4

### Background

A post office is a good example of a real-world environment in which numbers of different types can be found. Whole numbers and fractions are introduced. Numbers that occur in a greater variety of measurement situations can also be introduced. At this level, students should be encouraged to elaborate on the way the numbers are used. The writing and supporting reasons should be more sophisticated.

### Objectives

Students will be involved in discussing, describing, reading, and writing about whole numbers to thousands, decimal fractions to hundredths, and common fractions.

### Directions

1. Reproduce a copy of the activity sheet for each student.

2. Generally discuss the pictures of the things you might see at a post office. Ask the students to tell what they see or what they think is happening in each picture.

3. Tell the students to look at the pictures and find examples of the use of numbers. Spend enough time talking about the picture and other information about a post office so that students describe as many different ways as possible of using numbers. Challenge the students to tell how numbers could be used to—

• describe the size of a group—numbers less than 100, between 100 and 1 000, between 1 000 and 10 000, or greater than 10 000;

• identify locations—ZIP codes, street numbers on addresses;

• represent fractions—on weights; and

• express measurements—weight, volume, time, money, and so on.

4. Read the directions at the bottom of the sheet with the class. The students can then work independently or in small groups to complete the activities.

5. Select some examples of the written descriptions to read to the whole class.

### Extensions

1. Ask the students how numbers are used to describe length at the post office. They could visit or write the post office to find out the restrictions on the length of packages. They should then visualize the size of a package that might fit the restrictions.

2. Discuss the number 1 000. Ask the students to give different ways to describe it or think of it. For example, "About one thousand girls and boys attend our school" or "I take more than one thousand steps to walk around the edge of the playground." Have the students work in pairs to make up real-world questions about the post office. The answer to each question must be 1 000.

### Family activity

See "Numbers at Home" on page 112.

---

**Applicable Standards**

• **Communication**

• **Connections**

• **Number Sense and Numeration**

• **Fractions and Decimals**

---

*Prepared by* Calvin Irons *and* Rosemary Irons
*Edited by* Francis (Skip) Fennell

Name_____

# Post-Office Numbers

### New Stamps

$0.29    $0.50    $0.75

$1.00    $2.00    $5.00

Mail Holiday Cards by
10 December 1991

### Surface

| Weight | U.S. | Asia | Oceania |
|---|---|---|---|
| 1 oz. | $0.29 | $0.40 | $0.45 |
| 2 oz. | $0.52 | $0.80 | $0.90 |
| 3 oz. | $0.75 | $1.20 | $1.35 |
| 4 oz. | $0.98 | $1.60 | $1.80 |
| 5 oz. | $1.21 | $2.00 | $2.25 |

## Post Office Shop

| Boxes | Envelopes | Tubes |
|---|---|---|
| Cubic $0.80 | Small $0.50 | 200 mm $1.40 |
| Small rectangular $1.10 | Medium $1.00 | 300 mm $1.80 |
| Large rectangular $1.70 | Large $1.50 | 500 mm $2.20 |
| | Extra large $2.00 | |

Prestamped holiday postcards—$0.20 each
Prestamped holiday cards—$0.25 each

## Nonstandard Articles

(Large letters, small packets, books, business papers, merchandise)

| Charge per Article | Surface | Air |
|---|---|---|
| Up to 2 oz. | $0.65 | $0.75 |
| Over 2 oz. up to 6 oz. | $1.50 | $1.70 |
| Over 6 oz. up to 10 oz. | $3.00 | $3.30 |
| Over 10 oz. up to 16 oz. | $4.50 | $4.90 |
| Over 16 oz. | $5.50 | $6.00 |

1. Pick one number from the post-office scenes.
2. Write a description of how that number is used. Use the other side if more space is needed.

_____

_____

_____

From the *Arithmetic Teacher*, December 1991

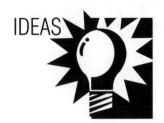

# Cut to Create

## LEVELS K–2

### Background

In this activity, students are involved in experimenting to cut a rectangular region into four triangular regions. The students then extend their investigation to rearrange the four triangular regions to construct a larger three-sided or four-sided figure. Throughout the investigation, the students describe what they are doing, using terms that are familiar to them. The teacher should encourage discussion to clarify thinking and to introduce terms where necessary.

### Objectives

1. To create four triangular regions from a rectangular region and describe in oral and written form the process and the result

2. To investigate informally the properties of a rectangle

### Materials

• Colored or construction paper on which you have duplicated a copy of the activity sheet "Cut to Create" for each student

• A pair of scissors for each student

• Paste for each student

• A ruler or other straightedge for each student

### Directions

1. Distribute a "Cut to Create" activity sheet to each student.

2. Read the directions on the activity sheet together with the students. At the same time, copy the directions on the chalkboard. Clarify what is meant by cutting the rectangular region into four triangular regions.

*Prepared by* Calvin Irons *and* Rosemary Irons
*Edited by* Francis (Skip) Fennell

3. Have the students cut out the rectangular region on the activity sheet.

4. Ask the students to suggest different ways in which they could cut the rectangular region into four triangular regions without using a ruler. In the discussion, encourage the students to use their own language to describe how they will cut the rectangular region; for example, "Cut along the slanted lines (diagonals)" or "Fold in half and then in half again from corner to corner." Some methods that could be used are shown in figure 1.

---

**FIGURE 1**

---

5. Refer to the directions on the chalkboard to complete the steps. Encourage the students, working independently or in pairs, to experiment to construct a larger triangular region or a different-looking four-sided figure using all the four smaller triangular regions. They can then paste their completed figure onto the activity sheet.

6. On a separate piece of paper, the students can work independently to write a draft description of what they did.

After editorial assistance from the teacher, the students can write a final version of the description on the activity sheet. Display the completed figures and descriptions on a bulletin board.

### Extensions

1. As an ongoing activity, challenge the class to find all the different three-sided and four-sided figures that can be made for each method of cutting the rectangular region into four triangular regions. On the bulletin board, make a chart of the original rectangular region cut into triangular regions and the methods suggested by the students for constructing new figures. Some examples are shown in figure 2.

2. Repeat the steps for this activity, but have the students cut the original rectangular region into eight triangular regions.

### Family activity

See "Making a Puzzle" on page 114.

---

**FIGURE 2**

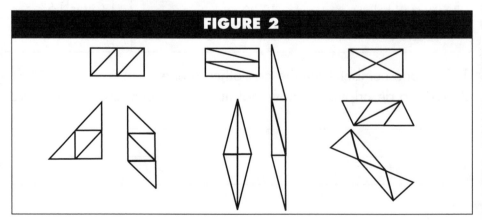

---

# Cut to Create

1. Cut out this rectangular region.
2. Think about different ways to make four triangular regions from this rectangular region. Do some folding to test your ideas. Then cut the rectangular region into four triangular regions.
3. Move around the four triangular regions to make different figures.

Paste in this space the best figure you made.

Write what you did to make different figures.

_____

_____

_____

From the *Arithmetic Teacher*, November 1991

# IDEAS

# Create a New Figure

## LEVELS 3–4

### Background

In this activity, students are involved in experimenting to cut a rectangular region into four specified pieces—a rectangular region, a square region, and two triangular regions. The students then extend their investigation to rearrange the four pieces to construct a larger figure. Throughout the investigation, the students describe what they are doing, using terms that are familiar to them. The teacher should encourage discussion to clarify thinking and to introduce terms where necessary.

### Objectives

1 . To create a new figure from four figures cut from a rectangular region and describe in oral and written form the process and the result

2. To investigate informally the properties of squares, other rectangles, and triangles

### Materials

• A copy of the activity sheet "Create a New Figure" for each student

• Construction paper for each student

• A pair of scissors for each student

• A ruler for each student

• Paste for each student

### Directions

1. Distribute a copy of the activity sheet to each student.

2. Read the directions on the activity sheet together with the students. Clarify any questions they might have.

3. Give each student a sheet of construction paper. Have the students cut out a rectangular region of approximately the same size as that shown on the activity sheet.

4. Ask the students to suggest ways in which they could cut the rectangular region into the four pieces. In the discussion, encourage the students to use their own language to describe how they will do the cutting. Discuss how the students know the pieces fit the criteria by pointing out and describing the special features of each figure; for example, "We will need to measure so that the *sides of the square are of the same length.*"

5. Encourage the students to experiment to construct a new figure with the four pieces. They should try to construct a figure whose name they know. They can then paste the figure onto the activity sheet.

6. The students can work independent-ly to write a description of what they did. Display on a bulletin board the completed figures and descriptions.

### Extension

Have the students repeat the activity using rectangles with the following dimensions: 6 cm × 12 cm, 6 cm × 15 cm, and 6 cm × 18 cm. For each rectangular region, have the students tell how they would decide to cut the four pieces.

### Family activity

See "Making a Puzzle" on page 114.

---

### Applicable Standards

• **Problem Solving**

• **Communication**

• **Geometry and Spatial Sense**

---

*Prepared by* Calvin Irons *and* Rosemary Irons
*Edited by* Francis (Skip) Fennell

# Create a New Figure

1. Use construction paper or some colored paper to cut out a rectangle about this size.
2. Cut the rectangular region into a square region, a rectangular region that is not a square region, and two triangular regions.
3. Use the four pieces to make a new figure.
4. Experiment to make different figures.

Paste your best figure here.

Write what you did to make the new figure.

_____

_____

_____

_____

From the *Arithmetic Teacher*, November 1991

# IDEAS

# What's the Weather?

## LEVELS K–2

### Background

These activities focus on studying a graph that reports the number of students who wore sweaters to school each day during one week. The information is shown in a pictograph. The students are asked to discuss and describe the information and then answer the questions on the basis of the given information. They are encouraged to write explanations to defend their answers.

### Objectives

To describe and explain information displayed in a pictograph and to make written predictions from it

### Directions

1. Reproduce a copy of the activity sheet for each student.

2. Have the students read the title of the graph and the words and numbers along the bottom and the side of the graph. The students should give their interpretation of the information in the graph.

3. Have the students describe the information in the body of the graph.

4. Read and discuss question 1. Ask the students to tell why—

- the number of sweaters on Monday was small,
- the number of sweaters increased on Tuesday, and
- the number of sweaters decreased on Wednesday.

Allow enough time in the discussion for every student in the group to offer a suggestion. The students can also ask their own questions about the graph and select other members of the class to answer their questions.

5. Have the students complete question 2. They should prepare a draft version on another sheet of paper and have the draft edited before writing the final version on the activity sheet. Ask the students to share their explanations.

### Extensions

1. Every day for a week, collect some information that depends on the weather (the number of sweaters, sweat shirts, coats, etc., worn to school) similar to the data shown on the activity sheet. Construct a graph and discuss how to label the information. Have the students make up some questions about the graph and then ask another class to answer the questions.

2. Construct a temperature graph covering the same period of time as the graph in extension 1. Look at the information in the two graphs and discuss any relationships; for example, when the temperature was between 50 degrees and 60 degrees, about half the class wore coats or sweaters.

---

### Applicable Standards

- **Connections**
- **Number Sense and Numeration**
- **Concepts of Whole-Number Operations**
- **Statistics and Probability**

---

*Prepared by* Calvin Irons *and* Rosemary Irons
*Edited by* Francis (Skip) Fennell

# What's the Weather?

Monday

Tuesday

Wednesday

Thursday

Friday

| 1 | 2 | 3 | 4 | 5 | 6 | 7 | 8 | 9 | 10 | 11 |

Number of Students Who Wore Sweaters to School

Use the graph to answer the following questions for the eighteen students in the class:

1. Why do you think the number of sweaters changed each day? _____

2. What was the weather like on Tuesday?_____

   Explain your response. _____

3. Do you think that someone needed to wear a sweater on Saturday? _____

   Why or why not? _____

4. On which day did the students wear two fewer sweaters than on Thursday? _____

5. How many more sweaters were worn on Wednesday than on Friday? _____

6. On which days did more than half the students wear sweaters?_____

From the *Arithmetic Teacher*, October 1991

# IDEAS

# Numbers and Me

## LEVELS K–3

### Background
This activity focuses on numbers that are familiar to students. The activity sheet serves as a way to introduce students to the teacher and to one another.

### Objective
To identify and use numbers in a real-life setting and to interpret survey data

### Directions
1. Prior to the activity, ask each student to bring in a recent photograph of herself or himself to mount on the activity sheet.

2. Reproduce a copy of the activity sheet for each student.

3. Have the students fill in the personal information up to the "Class Numbers Project" section.

4. Direct the students to fill in the "Class Numbers Project" information on the strip. Teachers may need to help the students determine their height and shoe size.

5. After the students have filled out the strip, have them cut it out, cut apart the data records, and place each data record in a box or give it to a small cooperative learning group.

6. After dividing the class into small cooperative learning groups, have each group analyze the data and report their data to the class.

7. As a class, determine from the data collected the correct responses to the information requested in step 4.

### Answers
Answers will vary.

### Applicable Standards
- **Connections**
- **Number Sense and Numeration**

### Extensions
1. Have the groups graph the results of their Class Numbers Project. Suggest the creation of bar or picture graphs.

2. Have students create and solve word problems about their "Numbers and Me" data. Problems should be shared with the class.

### Extension answers
Answers will vary.

### Family activity
See "How Tall Will I Be?" on page 116.

*Prepared by* Dianne Bankard *and* Francis (Skip) Fennell
*Edited by* Francis (Skip) Fennell

Name_____

# Numbers and Me

| Paste a recent photo here. |
| --- |

My name: _____

House or apartment number:_____

Phone number:_____

Grade:_____

Birthdate: _____

## More about Me

1. There are_____ people living in my home.

2. I have _____ brothers. I have _____ sisters.

3. I have_____ pets.

## A Class Numbers Project

| My shoe size | My age | My height in centimeters | My favorite number |
| --- | --- | --- | --- |
| | | | |

1. Fill in the information requested on the strip above.

2. Cut out the strips and place each section of the strip in a box or give it to your group.

3. Each group should review and explain the information they have collected.

4. As a class decide the following:

*Shoe size*
The most common shoe size_____
The largest shoe size_____
The smallest shoe size_____
*Age*
The oldest and youngest ages on the strips _____ and _____
The most common age_____
*Height*
The tallest and shortest heights on the strips_____ and _____
The height of most of the students _____
*Number*
The most common favorite number of the students_____
The least common favorite number of the students_____

From the *Arithmetic Teacher*, September 1991

IDEAS

# Survey of Hair and Eye Colors

## LEVELS 2–4

### Background

This activity involves data collection and interpretation through the use of a survey. The activity serves as an introduction to statistics.

### Objective

To collect, organize, and interpret data

### Directions

1. Reproduce a copy of the activity sheet for each student.

2. Give the students an opportunity to collect hair- and eye-color data from twenty students. The actual collection of these data might be best conducted as an after-school activity.

3. Make sure the students describe the people who participated in their survey. Discuss the importance of describing the source (sample) of the data collected.

4. As a class, discuss the completed surveys. Ask the students to discuss the most and least common hair and eye colors, as determined by the surveys.

5. Define a prediction as an attempt to describe the future, usually on the basis of data that have been collected. Discuss this process with the class. Explain that each day the TV weather reporter makes a prediction about the weather. Ask for responses to item 3, which asks for a prediction, based on the survey data, of the eye and hair colors of the next student to enter the classroom. Discuss the predictions with the class.

6. Determine the number of students with brown hair when five samples are combined, thus making a 100-student sample. The size of this sample allows immediate decimal representation. Ask the students to represent in fractional form the number of students with brown hair.

7. On the basis of the 100-student (combined) sample, discuss whether students are more likely to have brown eyes or blond hair. Ask students to give reasons for this likelihood.

### Answers

Answers will vary. For number 7, students in most populations would be more likely to have brown eyes than blond hair.

### Applicable Standards

- **Connections**
- **Statistics and Probability**
- **Fractions and Decimals**

### Extensions

1. Have students create a bar or picture graph of their results.

2. Have students represent the results of the combined surveys (100 responses) as decimals and percents, then suggest that this information be multiplied by 360 degrees to determine the size of each section of a circle graph that would represent the colors of hair and of one that would represent the colors of eyes. Then have the students create circle graphs to display the combined results. Discuss the completed graphs with the class, and then display them.

### Extension answers

Answers will vary.

### Family activity

See "How Tall Will I Be?" on page 116.

*Prepared by* Dianne Bankard *and* Francis (Skip) Fennell
*Edited by* Francis (Skip) Fennell

Name_____

# Survey of Hair and Eye Colors

Directions: Complete this survey by interviewing 20 students from your school. You may include your-self. Use tally marks to collect your data.

Describe the 20 students surveyed (grade level, school, etc.):

_____

_____

### Hair Color

|  | Tally Marks | Total |
|---|---|---|
| Black |  |  |
| Brown |  |  |
| Blond |  |  |

### Eye Color

|  | Tally Marks | Total |
|---|---|---|
| Brown |  |  |
| Blue |  |  |

Complete the following:

1. Which hair color is most common?_____ Least common?_____
2. Which eye color is most common? _____ Least common?_____
3. On the basis of your survey, predict the eye color and hair color of the next student to walk into your classroom. _____

   Explain how you arrived at your prediction._____

   _____

4. Combine your survey results with those of four other groups so that you have a survey of 100 students. Using a fraction or a decimal, express the number of brown-haired students compared with the total number of students._____

5. In the 100-student survey, do more students have brown eyes or blond hair? _____

From the *Arithmetic Teacher*, September 1991

# IDEAS

# Favorite Television Programs

## LEVELS 1–4

### Objective

Students conduct a survey to gather data about favorite television programs and then display the data in a chart. Students study their data and write about their conclusions.

### Materials

- A copy of a weekly television program guide for each group
- A copy of "Favorite Television Programs" for each student
- Large paper or poster board for making large graphs of the group's data

### Directions

1. Ask students questions like these, discussing their responses as a class:

- How do you think television networks decide which programs to show?
- Do you have a favorite television program for Monday? Is your favorite the same for every day?
- How could you go about finding out children's favorite Monday program?

(Discuss various methods for conducting a survey, including the use of a questionnaire and interviews. Ask how many children will have to be surveyed to make the data useful.)

2. Distribute copies of "Favorite Television Programs" and discuss its contents.

3. Place students in groups (seven groups—one to gather information for each day of the week—is an ideal number). Discuss desirable group behaviors.

4. Give each group a copy of a weekly television guide. Direct students to select a day of the week for their survey, working with the groups to see that each day is covered by only one group.

5. Discuss with each group the methods they could use to conduct their sur-

vey. Three important decisions must be made by each group: (1) whom to survey, (2) how to determine the data choices, and (3) which survey technique to use (written questionnaire or interview).

*Whom to survey.* It is important for students to discuss how many people they need to survey and how they are to select those people. One convenient method is to have each group survey students in a different class. This method avoids the logistical problem of groups in the class attempting to survey each other. Another method is to survey children in their neighborhoods after school.

*Determining the data choices.* Students must decide how they are going to get their subjects to make choices. One way is to ask them to name their favorite television program or their favorite program for a given night. It may, however, be difficult to remember the choices for a particular evening. Consequently, students may prefer first to have the group review the weekly television program guide and list six to ten programs for that evening. Then the students can show or read the list to the people being surveyed and ask them to select their favorite from those listed.

*Survey technique.* Two survey methods that work well for students are a written questionnaire that is completed by the subjects and an interview with subjects. If only a few people are being surveyed, the interview works well. If a large number of people are being surveyed, a written questionnaire, such as the one in figure 1, works well.

### Extensions

1. Distribute graphing materials so that each group can make a large graph to display their data. Data for different days could be compared and similarities and differences discussed.

2. Compare the data to Nielsen's cur-

rent lists of favorite programs, which are published weekly in the entertainment sections of larger newspapers.

3. Data on favorite types of programs could be collected through questionnaires or interviews. Programs can be categorized by type, such as cartoon, comedy, quiz show, sports, news, and so on. Weekly television program guides could be analyzed to derive data on the frequency of various types of network programs.

4. Data on favorite television characters could also be collected. Further, as television programs are watched at home, students could record information about the sex, age, and occupation of the characters. The data could be analyzed to determine whether television portrays the number of males, females, and children in proportion to the number in the real world.

### Family activity

See "Television at Home" on page 117.

---

### Applicable Standards

- **Communication**
- **Number Sense and Numeration**
- **Statistics and Probability**

---

## FIGURE 1

**Survey Questionnaire**
Draw a circle around your favorite Monday television program.

"The Candy Bears"

"Superdog"

"The Family Next Door"

"Time Tunnel"

"The Birthday Party"

"What Do You Know?"

---

*Prepared and edited by* Sharon L. Young

Name_____

# Favorite Television Programs

Work in a group.

1. Pick a day of the week and think about this question: What television program on that day of the week is the favorite of children? Make a survey to find out. Record the data in the chart.

**Favorite Television Program on** _____
(Day of the week)

| Television show | Tally marks | Number |
|---|---|---|
|  |  |  |
|  |  |  |
|  |  |  |
|  |  |  |
|  |  |  |
|  |  |  |
|  |  |  |
|  |  |  |
|  |  |  |
|  |  |  |
|  |  |  |

2. Write two true sentences about the results of the survey.

_____

_____

_____

_____

3. Tell what you did to find the favorite television program for the day you chose.

_____

_____

_____

_____

From the *Arithmetic Teacher*, May 1991

# Pizza-Topping Combinations

## LEVELS K–4

### Objective

Students explore the mathematical idea of combinations of two items. They record their results by cutting and pasting the various combinations.

### Materials

• . Scissors and paste
• A copy of "Pizza-Topping Combinations" for each student

### Directions

1. Ask students to imagine that they are working in a pizzeria that offers four different toppings: pepperoni, mushrooms, sausage, and green pepper. Their job is to put the toppings on the pizza. If they always put two toppings on each pizza, how many different pizzas can they make? What combinations are possible? Let students discuss possible answers.

2. Distribute copies of the "Pizza-Topping Combinations" activity sheet, scissors, and paste to each student. Discuss the directions with them. Students can work independently, in pairs, or in groups.

3. Some students may need assistance. Teachers could ask the students first to find cutout pictures of two different toppings and paste them onto one of the empty pizzas. Continue having the students paste other combinations.

4. After the activity sheet is completed, students can share their results.

### Extensions

1. Ask students to determine the number of pizzas of each of three sizes (large, medium, and small) that would be required to serve pizza to their class. The three sizes yield the following numbers of servings: large—six children; medium—four children; small—two children.

2. Obtain pizzeria menus and have students compute prices for pizzas with various combinations of toppings.

### Answers

Six different combinations are possible, as shown in figure 1. Note that the order of the combinations can vary.

---

**FIGURE 1**

## Possible combinations of two toppings

---

### Applicable Standards

• **Problem Solving**
• **Number Sense and Numeration**
• **Concepts of Whole-Number Operations**

### Extension Answers

1. Answers will vary. The following chart indicates the range of possible answers for a class of thirty students:

| Small pizzas | Medium pizzas | Large pizzas |
|---|---|---|
| 15 | 0 | 0 |
| 13 | 1 | 0 |
| 11 | 2 | 0 |
| 10 | 1 | 1 |
| 9 | 3 | 0 |
| 9 | 0 | 2 |
| : | : | : |
| : | : | : |
| 1 | 1 | 4 |
| 0 | 0 | 5 |

### Family activity

See "Pizza at Home" on page 118.

---

*Prepared and edited by* Sharon L. Young

# Pizza-Topping Combinations

In how many ways can you put two different toppings on a pizza? Cut along the dashed lines and paste the topping pictures on the pizzas to show the ways.

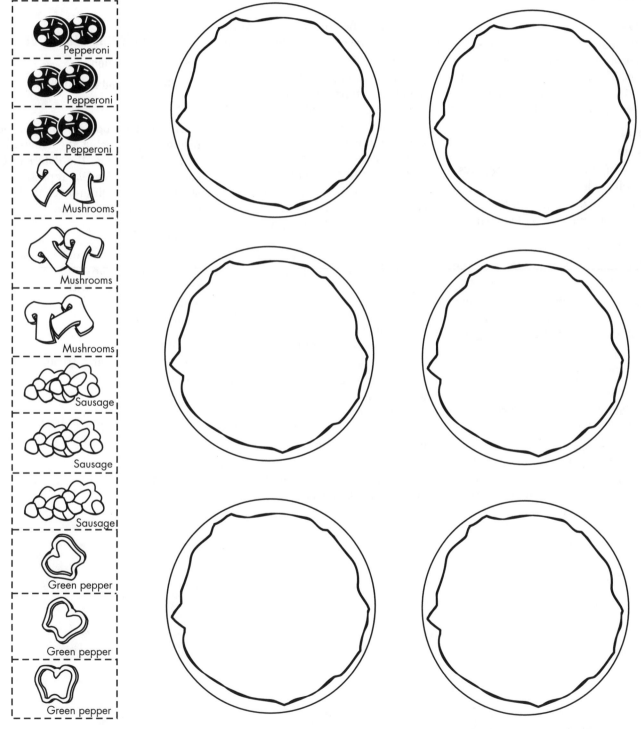

From the *Arithmetic Teacher*, April 1991

IDEAS

# Favorite Pizza Toppings

## LEVELS 1–4

### Objective

Students make a bar graph to display information about their favorite pizza toppings. The graph is then discussed, and students ask questions that can be answered by analyzing the graph.

### Materials

- Crayons
- A copy of "Favorite Pizza Toppings" for each student
- A copy of the "Pizza Data Sheet" on page 99 for each group of students

### Directions

1. Ask students such questions as the following and discuss their responses:

- When you order pizza, do you or your family order a plain cheese pizza or do you like to eat pizza with toppings on it?
- What kinds of toppings do you order?

2. Distribute copies of the "Favorite Pizza Toppings" activity sheet to students and discuss its contents.

3. Divide the class into groups of four to six students. Discuss group behaviors: help one another, disagree in an agreeable way, listen to others in your group, take turns, and so on.

4. Explain to the students that various methods can be used to collect the data to complete the graphs.

- In each group, students can ask about each topping in turn and raise their hands to indicate their choices. After the raised hands have been counted, each student in the group can color the appropriate number of pictures for that topping.
- Students can write their two choices separately on two slips of paper. The papers for students in a group can be combined, and then a student can read aloud each choice as the group members color the appropriate picture.

5. After the graphs have been completed, have each group study its graph and make some observations about the data.

6. Distribute a copy of the "Pizza Data Sheet" to each group of students. Discuss with students the data about favorite toppings, noting that pepperoni is the most popular topping.

7. Next, ask students to write some sentences comparing their results with the results on the data sheet.

### Applicable Standards

- **Communication**
- **Statistics and Probability**

8. Give each group time to report on its results, emphasizing the comparisons with the data from the data sheet. As each group makes its report, discuss similarities and differences in the findings of the various groups.

### Extension

Make a survey of favorite toppings for different age groups. Adults' responses could be compared with those of fourth and first graders to see if favorites change with age.

### Answers

Answers will vary frrom group to group.

### Family activity

See "Pizza at Home" on page 118.

---

*Prepared and edited by* Sharon L. Young

Name_____

# Favorite Pizza Toppings

Work in a group. Ask each person in the group to choose two favorite pizza toppings from those listed in the graph. Finish this graph to show the number of people who chose each topping. Color one picture for each choice made.

**Favorite Pizza Toppings**

| Topping Choices | | | | | | |
|---|---|---|---|---|---|---|
| Extra cheese | | | | | | |
| Green pepper | | | | | | |
| Mushrooms | | | | | | |
| Onion | | | | | | |
| Pepperoni | | | | | | |
| Sausage | | | | | | |
| | 1 | 2 | 3 | 4 | 5 | 6 |

Number of People Choosing Each Topping

Compare your results with those on the "Pizza Data Sheet."
Write some sentences. Tell how the results are the same or different.

_____

_____

_____

_____

_____

From the *Arithmetic Teacher*, April 1991

# Thumbprint Graph

## LEVELS 1–3

### Objective

With assistance from an adult, students classify their thumbprints by type of pattern. They then determine if the two thumbprints are of the same type or different types, and with other students in their group, they graph the thumbprint data and write about their results.

### Materials

- A copy of the "Thumbprint Graph" activity sheet for each student
- A copy of the "Fingerprint Data Sheet" on page 101 for each student
- Black watercolor and a brush or a stamp pad inked with a dark color
- A magnifying glass
- Graphing supplies: graph paper or large sheets of paper or poster board and marking pens or crayons

### Directions

1. Ask students questions like these, discussing their responses as a class:

- What do you know about fingerprints?
- Have you ever had a copy of your fingerprints made?
- What are some uses for fingerprints?
- Do you think your fingerprints are the same as mine or different? Why?
- Do you think the fingerprints from all your fingers are the same or different? Why?

2. Distribute copies of the "Fingerprint Data Sheet" and discuss the pictures of the various patterns of fingerprints without going into great detail. Ask students such general questions as "Which fingerprint looks like it has a hill in the middle?" Discuss with students the idea that fingerprints are unique for every finger, which is why they are so important in identifying people.

3. Set up a fingerprint center in the classroom for the purpose of taking thumbprints of each student. The thumbprints should be placed directly onto a copy of the "Thumbprint Graph" activity sheet. The teacher or an adult helper should take the prints during one or more class sessions. As the prints are taken, assist students in identifying with the use of a magnifying glass each print to determine its pattern. Have the students record the type of pattern in item 1.

4. Place the students in groups of four to six students. Discuss group behaviors: help one another, disagree in an agreeable way, listen to others in your group, take turns.

5. In item 2 on the activity sheet, have students determine whether their thumbprints are of the same type or of different types.

6. Distribute graphing materials so that each group can make a large group graph to complete item 3. Group members could make their own copy on their individual sheet to take home.

### Applicable Standards

- **Problem Solving**
- **Communication**
- **Patterns and Relationships**

7. After the graphs have been completed, each group should study its graph and make some observations about the displayed data.

8. The data from the graphs can be grouped together to make a class graph.

### Extensions

1. Take a full set of fingerprints for each student. Label each print with its pattern. Then have students make individual graphs to show how many arches, loops, and whorls appear in their ten fingerprints. See the sample in figure 1.

2. Combine the data from extension 1 to make a class graph.

### Family activity

See "Fingerprints at Home" on page 119.

*Prepared and edited by* Sharon L. Young

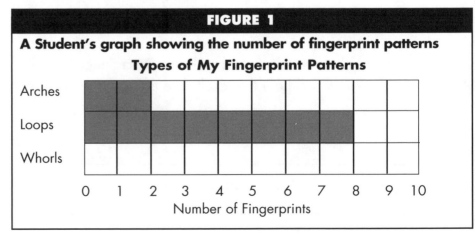

**FIGURE 1**

**A Student's graph showing the number of fingerprint patterns**

**Types of My Fingerprint Patterns**

# Thumbprint Graph

Work in a group.

1. Take your thumbprints in the boxes below. Write the type of pattern below each print. Use the "Fingerprint Data Sheet" to help you.

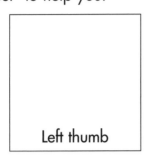

| Left thumb | Right thumb |

Pattern: _____        _____

2. Are your thumbprints both of the same type or are they of different types? Circle one answer.

               Same type                    Different types

3. Graph the answers for your group.

**Our Two Thumbprints**

| | | | | | | |
|---|---|---|---|---|---|---|
| Same type | | | | | | |
| Different Types | | | | | | |

0     1     2     3     4     5     6

Number of Students

4. Write about your results._____

_____

_____

_____

_____

_____

From the *Arithmetic Teacher*, March 1991

# Data Sheets

# IDEAS

## About the
# Television Data Sheet

Duplicate and send home with each student a copy of the "Television Data Sheet," along with a copy of "Television at Home," the family-activity sheet on page 117. Ask students to record the results of the home activities and then share the results with the class. The following information will help teachers and students interpret the television data.

1. The data collected from the A. C. Nielsen Company include cable-channel viewing. Additional data are available from Nielsen Media Research, 1290 Avenue of the Americas, New York, NY 10104. The data for viewing time per television-owning household include the total time a television is being viewed in a particular household, although that total time may comprise viewing times of several different people watching at various times of the day.

2. The data for viewing-time totals and achievement-test scores are the result of a 1982 study conducted by the California State Department of Education, which evaluated 500 000 sixth and twelfth graders.

3. *Prime time* is defined as 8:00 P.M. to 11 P.M. except in central-time and mountain-time zones, where it is 7:00 P.M. to 10:00 P.M.

4. The data on the distribution of program elements in children's Saturday programs in 1971 include two types of commercial announcements: those advertising products or publicizing political candidates and those promoting other programs, usually on the same network or channel. Noncommercial announcements include public-service announcements and station identification.

**Bibliography**

A. C. Nielsen Company. *Nielsen Report on Television 1990*. New York: Nielsen Media Research, 1990.

Barcus, F. Earle, with Rachel Wolkin. *Children's Television: An Analysis of Programming and Advertising*. New York: Praeger Publishers, 1977.

Bryant, Jennings, ed. *Television and the American Family*. Hillsdale, N.J.: Lawrence Erlbaum Associates, 1990.

Kaplan, Don. *Television and the Classroom*. White Plains, N.Y.: Knowledge Industry Publications, 1986.

Name_____

# Television Data Sheet

## Weekly viewing activity by age, 1989*

| Group | Average time per week |
|---|---|
| **Females** | |
| 12–17 | 21 h. 16 min. |
| 18–34 | 29 h. 16 min. |
| 35–54 | 31 h. 28 min. |
| 55+ | 41 h. 19 min. |
| **Males** | |
| 12–17 | 22 h. 18 min. |
| 18–34 | 24 h. 51 min. |
| 35–54 | 27 h. 52 min. |
| 55+ | 38 h. 22 min. |
| **Children (both sexes)** | |
| 2–5 | 27 h. 49 min. |
| 6–11 | 23 h. 39 min. |

## Nature of advertising for children's Saturday television programs, 1971 **

| Type of product | Percent of commercials |
|---|---|
| Toys | 23 |
| Cereals | 23 |
| Candies or sweets | 21 |
| Other foods | 23 |
| Vitamins or medicine | 1 |
| Other products | 9 |

## Distribution of program elements in Saturday children's programs, 1971**

| Program elements | Percent of time |
|---|---|
| Program content | 77.3 |
| Commercial announcements | |
| Commercial products | 15.5 |
| Program promotion | 3.3 |
| Noncommercial announcements | 3.5 |
| Other miscellaneous material | 0.4 |

## Viewing-time totals and achievement-test scores, 1982***

| Hours (h) of TV per weekday | Reading scores | Writing scores |
|---|---|---|
| 0 | 73 | 71 |
| $0 \le h < \frac{1}{2}$ | 75 | 74 |
| $\frac{1}{2} \le h < 1$ | 74 | 72 |
| $1 \le h < 2$ | 73 | 72 |
| $2 \le h < 3$ | 73 | 70 |
| $3 \le h < 4$ | 72 | 70 |
| $4 \le h < 5$ | 71 | 68 |
| $5 \le h < 6$ | 70 | 68 |
| $h \ge 6$ | 66 | 64 |

It is recommended that television be viewed from a distance greater than one meter (approximately 40 in.).

## Viewing time per television-owning household

| Year | Average time per day |
|---|---|
| 1950 | 4 h. 35 min. |
| 1951 | 4 h. 43 min. |
| 1952 | 4 h. 49 min. |
| 1953 | 4 h. 40 min. |
| 1954 | 4 h. 46 min. |
| 1955 | 4 h. 51 min. |
| 1956 | 5 h. 01 min. |
| 1957 | 5 h. 09 min. |
| 1958 | 5 h. 05 min. |
| 1959 | 5 h. 02 min. |
| 1960 | 5 h. 06 min. |
| 1961 | 5 h. 07 min. |
| 1962 | 5 h. 06 min. |
| 1963 | 5 h. 11 min. |
| 1964 | 5 h. 25 min. |
| 1965 | 5 h. 29 min. |
| 1966 | 5 h. 32 min. |
| 1967 | 5 h. 42 min. |
| 1968 | 5 h. 46 min. |
| 1969 | 5 h. 50 min. |
| 1970 | 5 h. 56 min. |
| 1971 | 6 h. 02 min. |
| 1972 | 6 h. 12 min. |
| 1973 | 6 h. 15 min. |
| 1974 | 6 h. 14 min. |
| 1975 | 6 h. 07 min. |
| 1976 | 6 h. 18 min. |
| 1977 | 6 h. 10 min. |
| 1978 | 6 h. 17 min. |
| 1979 | 6 h. 28 min. |
| 1980 | 6 h. 36 min. |
| 1981 | 6 h. 45 min. |
| 1981–82 | 6 h. 48 min. |
| 1982–83 | 6 h. 55 min. |
| 1983–84 | 7 h. 08 min. |
| 1984–85 | 7 h. 07 min. |
| 1985–86 | 7 h. 10 min. |
| 1986–87 | 7 h. 05 min. |
| 1987–88 | 6 h. 59 min. |
| 1988–89 | 7 h. 02 min. |

* Source: A. C. Nielsen Co. (1990)
** Source: F. Earle Barcus, *Children's Television* (1977)
*** Source: *San Francisco Chronicle,* 21 July 1982

From the *Arithmetic Teacher,* May 1991

# IDEAS

## About the
## Pizza Data Sheet

### Directions

The data sheet should be duplicated and used with one of the classroom activity sheets and the take-home family-activity sheet on page 118. Send home a copy of the data sheet, along with a copy of "Pizza at Home," which encourages the family's involvement. Ask the students to record the results of the take-home activities and then to share the results with the class.

The following information will help teachers and their students interpret some of the data.

1. The data for the "Top Ten Kids' Foods" chart come from a recent survey of families conducted by the Gallup Organization. The in-home survey asked parents of three- to eleven-year-olds to list their children's top ten mealtime preferences from a preselected list of foods. The survey reached a sample of 258 adult men and women in the United States. The results indicate that pizza was selected by 82 percent of the sample but that the grilled-cheese sandwich was selected by only 22 percent of the sample. Younger pupils can be assisted in understanding the data by an informal explanation of the idea of percent, such as the following: "Out of one hundred kids, eighty-two would list pizza as a favorite food."

Teachers may wish to point out to older students that although cheeseburgers and macaroni and cheese are ranked as the fourth and fifth choices, respectively, the same percents are given for both. Ask students how these statistics are possible or why both wouldn't be ranked fourth. Elicit the idea that these percents are most likely rounded and that many actual percents would have been rounded to 42 percent. For example, 41.51, 41.9, 42.1, and 42.49 would all round to 42.

2. A photograph of the world's largest pizza, mentioned in "Pizza Trivia," can be found in the 1989 and 1990 editions of the *Guinness Book of World Records*.

3. *Pizza Today* is a journal published by the National Association of Pizza Operators, P.O. Box 114, Santa Claus, IN 47579. Several items of data come from printed material supplied by the journal's staff.

4. The recipe for speedy pizza was adapted from *My First Cookbook* by Angela Wilkes (New York: Alfred A. Knopf, 1989).

### Extension

1. Students may wish to measure a length of 100 feet 1 inch on the playground to illustrate the size of the world's largest pizza.

2. Students may be interested in reading books with pizza themes. The bibliography suggests resources appropriate for students in elementary grades.

### Bibliography

Barbour, Karen. *Little Nino's Pizzeria.* San Diego: Harcourt Brace Jovanovich, 1987.

Basso, Bill. *The Top of the Pizzas.* New York: Dodd, Mead & Co., 1977.

Major, Beverly. *The Magic Pizza.* Englewood Cliffs, N.J.: Prentice Hall, 1978.

Martino, Teresa. *Pizza!* Milwaukee: Raintree Publishers, 1989.

Pillar, Marjorie. *Pizza Man.* New York: Thomas Y. Crowell Co., 1990.

"Poetry Page." *Instructor* 99 (September 1989): 58. Children's poems about pizza.

Rey, Margret, and Alan J. Shalleck, eds. *Curious George and the Pizza.* Boston: Houghton Mifflin Co., 1985.

IDEAS

Name_____

# Pizza Data Sheet

## Ten Top Kids' Foods
### (Ages 3–11 Years)

| | |
|---|---|
| Pizza ............................................ | 82% |
| Chicken nuggets ......................... | 51% |
| Hot dogs ..................................... | 45% |
| Cheeseburger .............................. | 42% |
| Macaroni and cheese ................. | 42% |
| Hamburgers ................................ | 38% |
| Spaghetti and meatballs............... | 37% |
| Fried chicken .............................. | 37% |
| Tacos........................................... | 32% |
| Grilled-cheese sandwiches ............ | 22% |

Source: Gallup Organization,1990

## Type of Crust Preferred

| | |
|---|---|
| Thin crust ......................... | 48% |
| Thick crust ..................... | 46% |
| No preference ................. | 6% |

Source: *Pizza Today*, 1990

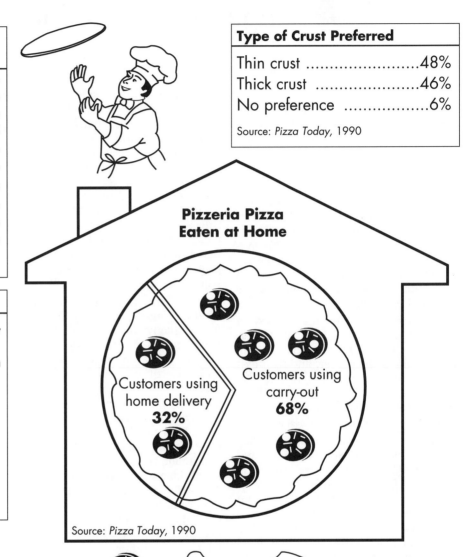

**Pizzeria Pizza Eaten at Home**

Customers using home delivery **32%**

Customers using carry-out **68%**

Source: *Pizza Today*, 1990

## Pizza Trivia

1. The world's largest pizza was built by Lorenzo Amato on 11 October 1987. It measured 100 feet 1 inch in diameter.

2. Americans eat 90 acres of pizza every day. The yearly average is 7 1/2 pizzas for each person.

3. Nearly 96 percent of all Americans now eat pizza about 30 times a year.

Source: *Pizza Today*, 1990

## Recipe for Speedy Pizza

### Ingredients

Pinch of salt
3 tablespoons butter
3 to 4 tablespoons milk
3/4 cup self-rising flour
1 8-ounce can pizza sauce
1/4 cup shredded cheese
Toppings of choice

### Directions

1. Preheat oven to 425°F, or 220°C.
2. Put flour, salt, and butter in mixing bowl.
3. Cut butter into small pieces.
4. Rub butter into the flour until the mixture looks like bread crumbs.
5. Add the shredded cheese and milk to the flour mixture. Mix until a smooth ball of dough forms.
6. Divide the dough in half and make each half into a ball. Roll each ball flat. Place on a baking sheet.
7. Spoon the pizza sauce over the dough.
8. Bake 15–20 minutes until edges are golden brown.

Source: Adapted from *My First Cookbook*, 1989

## Favorite Toppings
### (in Order of Preference)

Pepperoni
Mushrooms .
Extra cheese
Sausage
Green pepper
Onion

Source: *Pizza Today*, 1990

From the *Arithmetic Teacher*, April 1991

IDEAS

About the

# Fingerprint Data Sheet

## Directions

This data sheet should be duplicated and used with the class-activity sheet and the take-home family-activity sheet. The following information will help you and your students interpret the fingerprint data:

1. The classification of fingerprint-pattern types currently used by the Federal Bureau of Investigation (FBI) is based on the Henry system. This system recognizes three major categories of arches, loops, and whorls named according to the patterns made by the ridges of the fingers.

• *Arches.* The ridges in a *plain arch* (A) enter from one side of the finger, flow smoothly to form a curve resembling a hill in the center, and then exit the opposite side of the finger. The ridge pattern in a *tented arch* (T) is similar to a plain arch but forms a sharp upthrust that resembles a tent.

• *Loops.* Two pattern types are classified as loops: the *ulnar loop* (U) and the *radial loop* (R). In these two loop patterns, ridges enter from one side of the finger, curve to form a loop, and exit from the same side. These two loop patterns can cause some confusion because they are identified according to the hand from which the fingerprint is taken—left or right. With hands outstretched and palms down, as in taking fingerprints, one can identify two wrist bones in each arm. The ulna bone is at the outside edge of each wrist, nearest the little finger. The radius bone is at the inside edge of each wrist (see fig. 1). The loop fingerprints on each hand are identified according to whether they slope toward the ulna or the radius of that hand.

• *Whorls.* Four types of patterns are labeled as whorls. The ridges in the center of the plain whorl form a sort of whirlpool. Although the next two patterns have the word *loop* in their names, they are classified as whorls because the ridge lines do not enter

and exit on the same side of the finger. The *central-pocket loop* resembles a combination of an ulnar or radial loop and a plain whorl. The center of the *double-loop* pattern appears to form the letter S. Finally, the *accidental* pattern may bear some resemblance to the other patterns but not great enough to be classified as any of the others. Its ridges tend to enter from one side and exit on the opposite side, so it is classified as a whorl. When individual fingerprints are classified by symbols, all whorls are given the symbol W.

2. Seven basic ridge characteristics are used to identify or match fingerprints. It is unlikely that any one fingerprint has all seven characteristics; however, it is very likely that a fingerprint has multiples of one characteristic. The *ending ridge* is a ridge line that ends suddenly. A *bifurcation*, or two-pronged fork, divides into two continuing ridges. Similarly, a *trifurcation*, or three-pronged fork, divides into three continuing ridges. A *dot*, or *island*, is a small ridge section that stands by itself. An *enclosure* briefly divides into two then returns to being one ridge, resembling the eye of a needle. A *bridge* connects two ridges running roughly parallel to each other. A *hook*, or *spur*, divides into two, as in a birfucation or fork, but one of the ridges is very short and ends suddenly. These seven characteristics are used in court as evidence of matching fingerprints.

3. Loops are the most frequently occurring patterns or fingerprints, followed by whorls and finally by arches.

## Suggestions for taking fingerprints

The "Thumbprint Graph" activity sheet requires that students take their fingerprints. Here are some suggestions that will aid in taking fingerprints:

1. Police departments and sheriffs' offices typically are happy to send an "Officer Friendly" to classrooms to talk about their jobs. During such a visit, the officers could take fingerprints of students that would be kept by the students.

2. One method of taking fingerprints in the classroom uses a stamp pad inked with a dark color. Carefully press one finger at a time on the ink pad and then slide it over the surface of the pad. Press the finger onto white paper. Note that the "sliding" of the finger over the pad gives a much clearer print than just pressing the fingers on the pad. The latter approach tends to clump the ink.

3. Another method of taking fingerprints is to use black watercolor and a small paintbrush. Using the brush, carefully paint the surface of each finger and then press it onto white paper.

4. Teachers may find the following suggestions helpful in assisting students in taking their fingerprints:

• Practice taking your own prints first so that you can get a feel for what technique will work best with your own supplies.

• A clearer print can often be obtained by making more than one print from the same finger without reinking or repainting. If the ink is too heavy to get a clear print the first time, a second print can be made, resulting in a clearer image.

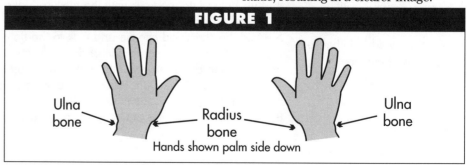

FIGURE 1

Ulna bone

Radius bone

Ulna bone

Hands shown palm side down

100

Name_____

# Fingerprint Data Sheet

## Types of Fingerprint Patterns

### Arches

Plain arch (A)

Tented arch (T)

### Loops

Right-hand ulnar loop (U)
or
Left-hand radial loop (R)

Right-hand radial loop (R)
or
Left-hand ulnar loop (U)

### Whorls (W)

Plain Whorl

Central-pocket loop

Double loop

Accidental

Source: Federal Bureau of Investigation, 1990

### Characteristics of Fingerprints

Ending ridge

Bifurcation
(Two-pronged fork)

Trifurcation
(Three-pronged fork)

Dot or island

Enclosure

Bridge

Hook or spur

### Frequency of Occurrence of Patterns

| | |
|---|---|
| Arches | 5% |
| Loops | 65% |
| Whorls | 30% |

Source: Federal Bureau of Investigation, 1990

From the *Arithmetic Teacher*, March 1991

# IDEAS

# Family Activities

# IDEAS

# Plastic Packaging

## FAMILY ACTIVITY

### Objective

To gather and graph data, to interpret the graph, to develop a recycling plan

### Directions

1. Show an item or two marked with a plastic recycling symbol. Use a disposable cup made of clear plastic or plastic foam, a plastic bag, or a plastic food package. Let the students find the symbol and note its number. Although plastic recycling numbers are voluntary, discuss why many manufacturers include them on new products. The recycling numbers occur in many places on plastic items and in no standard location.

2. Distribute a copy of the "Plastic Packaging" activity sheet to each student. Preview the directions. Suggest such qualities as color, thickness, and transparency for the students and their family members to notice in item 2 on the sheet. Ask the students to complete the activity sheets and bring them back to the classroom.

3. Ask the students to work in small groups to share their findings. Students can compile the total number of unmarked plastic items and the number with each marking. Have group representatives help to compile a chart or graph of the class's findings. Help students analyze the data, using the following questions:

- What marking occurred most often? Least often?

- Are more items marked or unmarked?

- Were any markings not easily found?

- Suppose that items with numbers 1 and 2 are "easy to recycle" and 6 and 7 are "very hard to recycle." Did we find more "easy" or "very hard" items? How can you tell?

- How could we use these results to predict what the number on another plastic item would be?

- What are some similarities and differences between your family's data and these large-group data?

4. Invite the students to share some of their families' suggestions about conserving and recycling plastics.

### Extensions

1. Students might copy and sketch the class results and report them to their families.

2. Students might repeat the activity at home, using more and different plastic products. They could then compare their predictions and graphs with the initial ones.

3. Students in grades 5–8 can interpret their families' and class's data using decimals and percents.

4. Students could use their families' data and make either a picture or a circle graph, for example.

IDEAS

# Plastic Packaging

Dear Family Members,

In school, your child has participated in activities in which facts were gathered about common products we use and ordinarily throw away. This activity will let you, as a family, look at plastic products and decide on some ways to prevent wasting plastics.

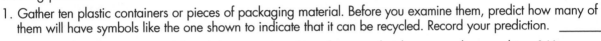

1. Gather ten plastic containers or pieces of packaging material. Before you examine them, predict how many of them will have symbols like the one shown to indicate that it can be recycled. Record your prediction. _____

2. Examine the plastic items. What did you notice about the ones that have recycling markings? You may have found a number on the item from 1 to 7. Items marked with 1's are the easiest plastics to recycle; those marked with 7's are the hardest to recycle. _____

_____

3. Talk and write about what you notice as you examine the plastic items marked with recycling numbers. If you find more than one item with the same number, are their similarities and differences obvious? Can you tell by looking which items have higher or lower numbers? Write some ideas. _____

_____

4. Fill in the graph to show the number of containers of each type.

### Markings on Plastic Containers

| No marking | |
|---|---|
| 1 | |
| 2 | |
| 3 | |
| 4 | |
| 5 | |
| 6 | |
| 7 | |

0  1  2  3  4  5  6  7  8  9  10

Number of Containers

5. Talk about your graph. Write down some things it shows. _____

6. On the basis of your graph results, can you predict whether the next plastic item you pick up will have a recycling number? If it has a number, what will the number be? _____

7. Plastics are common materials. Often we throw them away without thinking. If we conserved and recycled, much energy and money could be saved. Discuss your uses of plastics and the ways in which you dispose of the items. Could you reduce your use? Could items and products that are easily recyclable be substituted for those items that are harder to recycle? As a family, make and implement a plan to conserve plastic.

From the *Arithmetic Teacher*, September 1993

# Making Beds

## FAMILY ACTIVITY

### Literature
Myller, Rolf. *How Big Is a Foot?* New York: Atheneum Books for Children, 1972. ISBN 0-689-70306-6.

### Story Summary
The king demands that a bed be made using measures of his foot, but the carpenter uses his own foot as a measure instead, thereby causing the dimensions to be smaller than expected.

### Objective
Students explore the need for a standard unit of measure

### Materials
- *How Big Is a Foot?* by Rolf Myller
- Paper (to be used to trace nine footprints)
- Scissors

### Directions
1. Read the entire story aloud.

2. Tell the students that they will have the chance to explore some of the things that happened in the story with their family and friends at home.

3. Distribute an activity sheet to each student and ask the class to complete it and bring it back to school within an appropriate time of your choosing. Be sure to ask them to bring in their "footprints" as well as the activity sheet.

4. Discuss individual students' responses to the tasks described on the activity sheet.

### Extension
Use the students' "footprints" to explore the concept of "average." Was one size most common (mode)? When the footprints were arranged in order from smallest to largest, was one size in the middle (median)? In what different ways could we find the average size (mean)?

Discuss the problems that might occur if we used our footprints to graph our birth months. For example, a student born in January might tape one of his or her footprints end to end with those of others born in that month. Students born in other months should do the same for their month. Why might it be difficult to tell which month has the most birthdays by just looking at the height of the graph?

Name_____

# Making Beds

Dear Family Members,

We have been exploring instances of mathematics found in children's literature. We would appreciate your help in extending this activity by completing the exercises found on this activity page with your child. We will use this information and the story *How Big Is a Foot?* to discuss the importance of having a standard unit of measure when we communicate with others. Thank you and happy measuring!

The king in *How Big Is a Foot?* orders an apprentice to make a bed that is 3 (king's) feet wide and 6 (king's) feet long. But the apprentice uses his own foot to measure the bed. When the bed is finished, it's the wrong size. Why? Let's measure to find out.

Choose at least three people from your family and friends. Ask each person to do the following:

1. Trace his or her foot on a piece of paper.

2. Cut out the tracing carefully.

3. Make eight more copies of the footprint.

4. Place the footprints end to end on the floor to make two sides of a bed that is 6 footprints long and 3 footprints wide.

Are all the beds of the same size?_____
Whose footprints made the largest bed?_____
_____
Whose footprints made the smallest bed?
_____Are any
of the beds too small for any members of your
family?_____
Why do you think the ruler was invented? _____
_____
_____
_____

The preface of the book says, "To the wonderful metric system, without whose absence in this country this book would not have been possible."
What do you think the author means by this statement? _____
_____
_____
_____

From the *Arithmetic Teacher*, May 1993

Name_____

# Olympics on the Home Front

Dear Family Members,

Your child has been studying the Olympic Games, using measurement in mathematics class. You can hold your own "family olympics" by trying these three events.

## Dishcloth Toss

Have each member of the family estimate the distance he or she can throw a wet dishcloth and a dry dishcloth. Now throw the dishcloths. The person who is closest to the estimate wins.

| Family member's name | Estimate in feet | |
|---|---|---|
| | Wet cloth | Dry cloth |
| | | |
| | | |
| | | |
| | | |

Which cloth went farther—the wet one or the dry one? _____

Did everyone throw the same cloth farther?_____

What objects are about the same length as the distance of your dishcloth toss? _____

What objects are about half the length of your toss?_____

Who is the dishcloth-toss winner? _____

## Kitchen Cleanup

Each night one person cleans up the kitchen, including washing the dishes and sweeping the floor. Each family member should estimate how long he or she will take to clean the kitchen. Then use a clock to record the number of minutes it actually takes each person to clean up. The family member whose actual time is closest to the estimate wins.

| Family member's name | Time in minutes | |
|---|---|---|
| | Estimate | Actual |
| | | |
| | | |
| | | |
| | | |

Did you clean the kitchen faster than you estimated? ____

Whose time was closest to the estimate? _____

Name at least two other things you can do in the same amount of time as you took to clean up the kitchen._____

What can you do in twice the amount of time you took to clean up the kitchen? _____

_____

Who is the kitchen-cleanup winner? _____

## Book Balance

Find a book that weighs about one pound. Place the book on your head and walk for as long as you can while balancing it. Use a watch with a second hand to record the time in minutes and seconds. The winner is the person who balances the book the longest.

| Family member's name | Time in minutes and seconds |
|---|---|
| | |
| | |
| | |
| | |

Who is the book-balance winner? _____

Who is the overall "family olympics" winner for all three events?_____

From the *Arithmetic Teacher*, April 1992

Name_____

# Number Sense at Home

Dear Family Members,

Your child has been participating in classroom activities that involve building number sense—the understanding of numbers and their relationships. The activities below will help your child think about number relationships. They are designed for students to estimate sums close to 100 and monetary amounts close to $10.00.

## THE "100 THINK" GAME

*Object of the game:* To find two numbers that sum to close to 100 when added

*Materials:* Twenty index cards with the following numbers, one number per card:

22, 84, 18, 81, 5, 92, 47, 50, 79, 16, 36, 60, 29, 72, 41, 58, 15, 90, 3, 95

*Directions:* Mix up the index cards and turn them facedown. The first player turns over two cards at one time. If the sum of the numbers is 100 or close to 100 (upper 90s or low 100s), the player keeps the cards. If the sum of the numbers on the two cards is not close to 100, then the cards must be returned to the table facedown. The second player repeats the activity. Play continues until no more pairs can be made. The player with the most cards at the end of the game wins.

## THE "MONEY THINK" GAME

*Object of the game:* To find two monetary amounts that come close to $10.00 when added

*Materials:* Twenty index cards with the following monetary amounts, one amount per card:

$3.35, $7.01, $2.25, $6.80, $9.05, $1.10, $5.50, $4.25, $3.20, $5.80, $1.50, $8.00, $0.55, $8.75, $0.97, $8.50, $3.10, $7.25, $4.80, $5.10

*Directions:* Mix up the index cards and turn them facedown. The first player turns over two cards at a time. If the sum of the amounts is $10.00 or close to $10.00, the player keeps the cards. If the sum of the amounts on the two cards is not close to $10.00, then the cards must be returned to the table facedown. Play continues until no more pairs can be made. The player with the most cards at the end of the game wins.

From the *Arithmetic Teacher*, March 1992

Name_____

# Patterns at Home

Dear Family Members,

Geometric patterns and patterns in everyday life are the focus of our mathematical activities for the next week. We invite you to be part of these activities by discussing with your child different patterns found around your home and community.

You might ask, "What do you mean by *pattern*?" Our definition of *pattern* is the repetition of a geometric figure to cover an area in the home or outside the home. Some of you may have a tiled floor. Many times the tiled floor is made up of a number of square pieces put together in a pattern to cover the entire floor. Brickwork or wood floors around your house and brick streets in the community have a definite pattern. Aluminum or board siding creates a rectangular pattern on a house.

If you have a camera, you might take photographs of some of the patterns you find together and send them to school with your child. We shall display all the photographs for other students to enjoy. We shall also group the photographs according to the geometric figures used in the pattern. Patterns abound in the world around us.

Your child will be studying various patterns during the week. As a final lesson, we would like you and your child to design a new floor for a room in your house, dream house, or apartment. Let your child be your guide in this project. After you have designed the floor, your child should return the design to school, and we shall make a bulletin board of the various designs. We also invite you to come to school to see the various designs that parents and children have made for their final project.

# Numbers at Home

## FAMILY ACTIVITY

**Background**

This activity will extend the investigation of numbers in real-world situations to numbers in the home.

**Objective**

Students will work with their family to find examples of the use of numbers (whole numbers and fractions) in the home.

**Directions**

1. Reproduce a copy of the family-activity sheet for each student.

2. Have the students take the activity sheet home to complete it with their family. Encourage the students to bring the completed activity sheet back to school to discuss any interesting observations that they made.

Name_____

# Numbers at Home

Dear Family Members,

At school, we have been talking about various ways in which numbers are used. These discussions help your child understand different concepts of number. Clear concepts of number will help your child make estimates and solve problems.

The following activity can reinforce your child's understanding of number.

1. Look for ways in which numbers are used in your home.
2. Work with your child to find numbers used with appliances or in areas of the home.
3. For each example, ask your child to write how the number was used.

**Appliances**                                    **Areas**

Kitchen

Bedroom

Bathroom

From the *Arithmetic Teacher*, December 1991

# Making a Puzzle

## FAMILY ACTIVITY

### Background

The related "Ideas" activities encourage students to describe and record geometry activities involving cutting and rearranging rectangular regions. This family activity extends the investigation to a cutting activity that can be completed in the home.

### Objective

Students will work with their family to construct a puzzle from a familiar rectanglar region. The family members are encouraged to discuss with the child the steps that were followed.

### Directions

1. Reproduce a copy of the family-activity sheet for each student.

2. Have the students take the activity sheet home to complete it with their family. Encourage the students to bring to school the puzzles they constructed at home. Have the students explain or write a description of what they did.

Name_____

# Making a Puzzle

Dear Family Members,

In school we have been cutting out figures and moving them around. This visualization helps your child understand what is happening when he or she solves problems. We have been investigating and constructing new figures and making puzzles from a rectangular region.

   You and your child can continue these investigations by doing the following activity, which involves creating a jigsawlike puzzle.

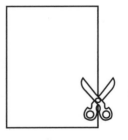

Use an empty cereal box.

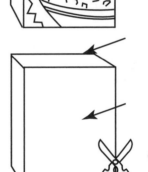

Have your child cut out the front and back panels of the box.

Cut two large sides.

Ask your child to cut one panel of the box into four figures, using the entire panel. Look away as your child cuts the figures.

Cut into four figures.

Use the other panel as a baseboard. Try to fit the four figures together to cover the baseboard.

Changing roles with your child, repeat the foregoing steps by using another cereal box.

From the *Arithmetic Teacher*, November 1991

Name_____

# How Tall Will I Be?

Dear Family Members,

Your child and his or her classmates have been using mathematics in class while collecting information and investigating data about themselves. The activities on this sheet allow you to work with your child to complete information about height expectancies and answer questions about the heights of family members. The table displays average heights for children; your family records might furnish data on your particular family. Other such resources as an encyclopedia, an almanac, or the *Guinness Book of World Records* can yield interesting related information. Have fun with these real-life mathematics activities.

**Average Height for Children**

| Boys | | Girls | |
|---|---|---|---|
| Age in years | Height in centimeters | Age in years | Height in centimeters |
| 2 | 96.2 | 2 | 95.7 |
| 4 | 103.4 | 4 | 103.2 |
| 6 | 117.5 | 6 | 115.9 |
| 8 | 130.0 | 8 | 128.0 |
| 10 | 140.3 | 10 | 138.6 |
| 12 | 149.6 | 12 | 151.9 |
| 14 | 162.7 | 14 | 159.6 |
| 16 | 171.6 | 16 | 162.2 |
| 18 | 174.5 | 18 | 162.5 |

Source: *Current Pediatric Diagnosis and Treatment 1987*, edited by C. Henry Kempe, M.D., et al. (Norwalk, Conn.: Appleton & Lange, 1987)

## Vital Statistics

My height at birth:_____;

   at age six:_____.

My age today is _____.

I am _____cm tall.

I am _____cm taller than I was at age six.

I am   taller   shorter   than average (circle one).

I predict that my height will be _____cm when I am fourteen.

I predict that my height will be _____cm in ten years.

## Predictions about Height

Use the table "Average Height for Children" to answer the following questions:

1. Would you say that most members of your family are tall or short?_____ Explain your answer.

_____

2. Ralph noted that he was 150 cm tall at age ten. Do you think he would be 300 cm tall at age twenty? ____Explain your answer. _____

3. Do you expect to be about average, taller than average, or shorter than average by age twenty?   ____Explain your response. _____

4. How likely are you to grow to be over 160 cm tall?_____Explain your answer. _____

_____

5. Make a bar graph comparing the heights of everyone living in your house. Order the heights according to the ages of the persons measured, beginning with the youngest.

From the *Arithmetic Teacher*, September 1991

IDEAS

Name_____

# Television at Home

(Refer to "Television Data Sheet" on page 97.)

Dear Family Members,

Your child has been using mathematics in class while collecting and investigating data about television. Three additional activities are suggested on this sheet. You and your child may want to do one or nore of them together. Check the accompanying data sheet to compare your data.

### How Far from the TV Screen Do You Sit?

Do you sit a safe distance from the screen? Measure to find the distances from the TV screen that you and others in your home usually sit. Compare your measurements with the recommendation on the data sheet.

### Keep a Family Viewing Log

For one week, keep a log of the times each person in your family watches television. Find the total viewing time for each person for that week. Compare the totals to those on the data sheet for the appropriate sexes and ages.

| MONDAY EVENING | JOHN | SANDRA | MORGAN |
|---|---|---|---|
| 5–6 p.m. | YES | No | YES |
| 6–7 p.m. | NO | No | No |
| 7–8 p.m. | YES | No | YES |
| 8–9 p.m. | YES | YES | NO |

### What Do You Do during Commercials?

Survey your family, friends, and neighbors about what they do during commercials. Record your results in a chart.

### Commercial Viewing and Listening

| Action | Tally | Number of people |
|---|---|---|
| Watch and listen | | |
| Watch only (Turn sound off) | | |
| Listen only | | |
| Neither watch nor listen (Leave room, etc.) | | |

From the *Arithmetic Teacher*, May 1991

117

Name_____

# Pizza at Home
(Refer to "Pizza Data Sheet" on page 99.)

Dear Family Members,

Your child has been exploring mathematical topics associated with data about pizza. This sheet suggests three different activities using ideas connected with pizzas. You and your child could select one or more of the activities to do together. Check the accompanying data sheet for survey data and for a recipe for making pizza.

Make pizza with an adult. Use your own recipe or the recipe for speedy pizza on the "Pizza Data Sheet." Be sure to measure all ingredients carefully.

Conduct a survey of some neighbors and friends. Pick one or more of these questions to use for your survey:

1. How many times a month or a year do you eat pizza?
2. Which type of pizza crust do you prefer—thin or thick?
3. How do you get your pizza?
   - Eat at pizzeria
   - Carry out from pizzeria
   - Request home delivery
   - Purchase frozen from grocery store
   - Make at home

Compare your data with those on the data sheet. Are your results similar?

In how many different ways can you share a whole pizza with another member of your family? Cut this pizza along the dashed lines so that you have six pieces. Share the six pieces in various ways and record on the chart the number of slices for each person.

_____     _____
(Your name)           (Family member's name)

_____             _____

_____             _____

_____             _____

_____             _____

_____             _____

_____             _____

From the *Arithmetic Teacher*, April 1991

Name_____

# Fingerprints at Home

(Refer to "Fingerprint Data Sheet" on page 101.)

Dear Family Members,

Your child has been using fingerprints to investigate such mathematical ideas as patterns in nature. This sheet shows several different activities that use fingerprints. You and your child could select one or more of the activities to do together.

You will need—

• a copy of the "Fingerprint Data Sheet,"

• a magnifying glass or a pair of reading glasses, and

• an ink pad or dark watercolors.

**Three Methods for Obtaining Prints**

Follow one of these methods to obtain prints:

1. Visit your local sheriff or police station and have your fingerprints taken. You will be given the copy.

2. Slide fingertips over an ink pad, then press onto white paper.

3. Use a small paintbrush to paint fingertips with dark watercolor paint, then press onto white paper.

*Note:* When taking your own prints, you may need to practice to obtain clear prints.

Take thumbprints of all family members, and label them with the name, left or right thumb, and the type of pattern (see the data sheet). In your family, whose thumbprints are of the same pattern as yours? Look at all the thumbprints you took. Which type of pattern occurs most often—arches, loops, or whorls?

Go to the library. Find books about fingerprints. Some science books and books about the body have such information.

Two of the thumbprints below are identical. Which are they? _____ and _____

Thumbprint A          Thumbprint B          Thumbprint C          Thumbprint D          Thumbprint E

   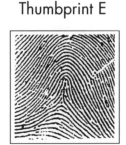

From the *Arithmetic Teacher*, March 1991